China And The United States: Beyond 2020

Asian Culture Press

First paperback edition August 2021

Edited by Janvi Chow

Cover art by Mengzhi Hu

Layout by Mengzhi Hu

Printed in the United States of America

Asian Culture Press
444 Alaska Avenue,
Suite #AZF046,
Torrance, CA 90503
United States

Abstract

This study mainly focuses on exploring how China and the United States, under a new historical context, would possibly engage with each other, and in what ways their interactions would have impacts on both the two countries and the world. More precisely, from a normative and theoretical perspective, this research tends to observe whether and how China-U.S. bilateral engagements could affect the core theories and values that have, in certain ways, guided the policy-making of and the relations among states over the past decades; and from a practical perspective, by taking numerous new phenomena such as the implications of the COVID-19 into account, it aims to foresee the possible impacts of the development of China-U.S. relations on the political, economic, social, and other aspects of activities of the two countries, and of the world to a larger extent. With the COVID-19 sweeping across the globe since around the beginning of 2020, and the serious repercussions led by it, many analysts already indicated that the implications of the Coronavirus pandemic could possibly last for some years to come. Overall, this project mainly aims to foresee a number of possibilities to be generated by China-U.S. interactions in the post-pandemic era.

Contents

Abstract

Acknowledgements

Introduction   1

Chapter 1. Values and Theories   9
   I. Rethink of the Realist Tradition-the "Thucydides
   Trap" Argument   11
   II. Liberal Values and the Liberal International
   Order: Limits and Future Direction   28

**Chapter 2. Major Power Relations, Global Governance, and
    World Order**   49
   I. Global Governance Is at A New Cross Road   51
   II. Prospects of China-U.S. Bilateral Engagements
   in the Future   64

**Chapter 3. China and the United States on the Coronavirus and
    Beyond**   99
   I. The Coronavirus, Non-traditional Security, and
   Ideology   101
   II. Practical Measures in Fighting the COVID-19
   Pandemic   111
   III. The Coronavirus, the United States, and the
   World   118

Chapter 4. China and the United States on Taiwan and Hong
    Kong   133
    I. On the Taiwan Local Election   135
    II. The U.S. Moves on the Taiwan Issue under the
    Trump Administration: Symbolic or Substantial? 142
    III. Commentary: A Public Opinion Poll and Its
    Relevance to the Future Cross-strait Relations   153
    IV.Commentary: China's National Security Law and
    the Practice of the "One Country, Two Systems"
    Principle in Hong Kong   157

Conclusion   165

References   167

Acknowledgement

I would like to take this opportunity to express my sincere appreciation to my then university teachers for their guidance and help in learning, to my dear friends for their understanding and patience, as well as to those whom I had closely worked with for their help, understanding, and support. Their names have been and will be remembered.

Gratefulness would also be given to a number of great people whose greatness has inspired me to carry on my work.

My gratitude would go to my parents as well for everything they have given me.

Introduction

Over the past decades, realism and liberalism have been two of the most important theories in international relations. On the one hand, they have been in a position of seeking to interpret states' past behaviour; and on the other hand, they have been playing a role of guiding states' policy-making in certain ways.

With the world stepping into the new century, a lot of new changes and phenomena have been taking place at the international stage. Certain limits and shortcomings of the two important theoretical traditions have appeared in relation to their functions of interpreting and guiding. There is no perfect theory all the time and under all conditions. Theories have been evolving. For the realist tradition, it has undergone a period from classical realism to neo-realism and further to neo-classical realism by adding new assumptions into the realist school in different stages. For the liberal school, it has developed from classical liberalism to neo-liberalism.

In the meantime, other schools of theories and values have emerged and been evolving as well alongside the changing environments and circumstances in both the regional and international dimensions. Among them, Marxism/neo-Gramscian, critical theory, constructivism, structuralism, feminism, post-modernism, and the green theory etc. have been the influential ones generally. It is worth emphasizing that the practice of Marxism in China has been developed to a new stage by being innovatively localized in line with China's internal conditions.

In order to avoid blindly applying certain theories and values under various new conditions, there should be a need to be rethinking some of them, in particular, the realist and liberal schools from a historical and critical perspective, as well as the power relations and structural frameworks facilitated by the two theoretical traditions. More precisely, the practical purpose for rethinking the theories is to make them help better understand the series of emerging phenomena and challenges, and further, better guide policy-making in the new era.

In addition to the above broader sentiment, with regard to the specific challenges and phenomena faced by the world in 2020, the coronavirus pandemic should be the number one challenge. Due to that, the year of 2020 was very unusual for the world. Till now, the pandemic situation across the world is still serious. With the COVID-19 sweeping through the world over the past year, fighting the virus has been one of the key priorities for almost all nations. Meanwhile, along with the process of combating the pandemic, a number of other core issues such as non-traditional security, ideology, governance model, as well as the economic, social, and political impacts of the pandemic on various countries have been come into discussions. The management of the coronavirus pandemic by China and the U.S. respectively as well as the different outcomes secured by the two countries have particularly generated a lot of debates.

To further extent, the diverse outcomes obtained by different countries in managing a series of crises since the beginning of the new century have revealed a fact that the world is approaching toward a new critical point in many ways, under which, various key actors are in need to seriously think about the future of a number of critical issues on the national, regional, and international levels - such as the values for guiding people's lives, the theories for directing policy-making, the functions of domestic systems, non-traditional security, power relations, global governance, globalization, and world order and so on.

Given the above background, this book bears three purposes:

First, rethinking the merits and limits of the two important schools, realism and liberalism;

Second, analysing China-U.S. interactions on a number of core issues mainly covering foreign and security affairs, economy and trade, technology, the coronavirus pandemic, Hong Kong, and Taiwan, as well as the impacts of China-U.S. engagements in these areas on the overall bilateral relations between the two countries and beyond;

And third, trying to think about a new alternative approach to facilitate the establishment of a new type of great power relations and of a new type of international relations on the one hand, and to pave the way for improving the global governance system and possibly forging a new world order on the other hand.

Chapter one consists of two articles focusing on the assessment of two schools of theories, realism and liberalism. The two schools of thoughts have significantly affected states' policy-making and international relations over the past decades. They will be analysed more from a critical and dialectical perspective. Criticism is not the purpose. The real purpose of reasonable debates and criticisms is to explore whether and in what possible ways the two schools of theories can be creatively understood and further be improved to better serve states' policy-making under various circumstances in the future.

Chapter two tends to outline the challenges faced by the world in the global governance sphere. In addition to that, given the fact that China-U.S. bilateral engagements in a number of areas would not only generate a big impact on the two countries but also on the world more broadly, this chapter would also attempt to explore the prospects of China-U.S. bilateral engagements in the future as well as their significance to both the two countries and the world. The purpose of doing this chapter is to seek an alternative approach to promote problem-solving between China and the U.S. and beyond, as well as to help enrich the theories and practices of a new type of international relations.

Chapter three concentrates on a list of recordings on the development of the coronavirus pandemic in the year of 2020, as well as on the measures and policies taken by the U.S. and China respectively at various development stages of the pandemic. Alongside the extraordinary efforts made by a number of countries in fighting the COVID-19 pandemic, other series of issues such as non-traditional security, ideology, and globalization trend etc. have been raised. These issues will be briefly discussed as well in this chapter.

Chapter four tends to analyse China-U.S.

interactions on China's internal affairs, mainly in relation to Hong Kong and Taiwan - more specifically, what moves the U.S. has taken toward Taiwan and Hong Kong, and how China has reacted, as well as the possible implications of the relevant moves and responses.

Chapter 1

Values and Theories

I. Rethink of the Realist Tradition - the "Thucydides Trap" Argument

Thucydides, who lived in ancient Greece around 2500 years ago, is the author of *History of the Peloponnesian War*, which recorded the conflicts between two Greek city-states Sparta and Athens. Thucydides's work set the foundation of the realist tradition.

It is assumed that the most well-known argument in Thucydides's masterpiece should be that the root cause of the great conflict between Athens and Sparta was the rising of Athens and the fear this caused in Sparta.

In other words, Athens and Sparta were caught in a security dilemma or security trap, which, as many have thought, made the war inevitable. Some also name the security trap as "Thucydides Trap".

Then to argue for the inevitability of the war between the two Greek city-states, some observers have intended to use a scenario of "Prisoner's Dilemma" to depict the security dilemma faced by the two Greek powers.

Here is a possible scenario of "Prisoner's Dilemma" - two criminal suspects jointly committed a crime, were arrested and put into two different cells of the same prison by the police. To make a fair charge, the police need to get enough information from them. The amount of information uncovered would directly lead to three possible results: If the two suspects all stay in silence, both of them would possibly get a lighter punishment; if one of them stays in silence while the other uncovers the criminal information, the one keeping in silence would be more heavily charged; if both of them choose to uncover their deeds, they would get the same degree of punishment. What is most likely to happen, under the pre-condition that there is no chance of communication between the two suspects, should be that both of them would attempt to cheat on the other in order to get a lighter punishment. Therefore, the two prisoners finally are trapped in a security dilemma, and this kind of dilemma cannot be overcome.

By connecting the scenario of "Prisoner's Dilemma" to the security situation faced by two states, an ultimate conflict between two states, as many may have maintained, would be inevitable.

The purpose of this analysis is to re-think of the "Thucydides Trap" argument by assessing whether it is appropriate to put an analogy between two states and two prisoners in terms of the dilemma faced by the two different groups; then it will try to understand the "Thucydides Trap" argument in today's world to examine whether and how it could be possible for state actors to surpass it.

To answer the above questions well, this piece assumes that the starting point is to re-check briefly of what had happened 2500 years ago during the Peloponnesian war among the Greek city-states, through which, to see whether there could be any limits and deflections in Thucydides's assessment on the root cause of war.

The Issue of "Fear" & the Root Cause of War

Thucydides argued that the rising of Athens and the fear it caused in Sparta made the conflict between them inevitable. This assessment would respectably propose a view that if there was a fear within Sparta by then, the same fear also existed inside Athens, as both powers wanted to maintain a balance of power among the Greek city-states, and both were afraid of losing that balance. A typical example to show how Athens was fearful of losing the balance was of its final decision to join the Corcyra's side against Corinth.[1] From Athens's perspective, if it failed to check Corinth and let the Corinthians take over Corcyra's navy, the balance of power could risk turning into a situation

13

against the Athenian power itself.[2]

Besides that, according to Donald Kagan's argument cited from Nye's book *Understanding International Conflicts*, Sparta was more fearful of war and of a slave revote than of the growing Athenian power, as 90% of Sparta's population were slaves, and a revote within Sparta had recently taken place in the year of 464 B.C.[3]

Thus, Thucydides's argument on the root cause of war didn't seem to be adequate. There should be more than just fear behind the conflicts between Athens and Sparta.

To better understand the cause of the Peloponnesian war, a list of historical events, which had briefly recorded the rising and breaking down of Athens, are worth noticing here.[4]

* After around half a century of war between Greece and Persia, in 449 B.C., Athens and Sparta and other Greek city-states jointly defeated the Persian power. Then Athens had enjoyed a long period of relatively peaceful time for developing itself; with the growing strength of it, Athens and a number of Greek city-states formed the Delian League; around the same period, Sparta and other series of city-states surrounding Sparta established a defensive alliance;

* In the year of 461 B. C., the first Peloponnesian war was

erupted, caused mainly by the growing tension between Athens and other city-states within the Delian League, as Athens had pressed them to pay taxes in exchange for receiving Athens's protection;

* In 445 B.C., the war between Athens and others was ended and followed with a 30-year truce;
* In 431 B.C., Athens ignored Sparta's warning and broke the truce made previously, then the second Peloponnesian war was broken out;
* In 421 B.C., another truce was signed between Athens and Sparta;
* In 413 B.C., Athens took its most serious adventure to attack Sicily, which had close linkages with Sparta; a conflict was unleashed between Athens and Sparta, and it was ended with a huge defeat of Athens; after that Athens had never re-gained its strength;
* After the defeat of Athens in 413 B.C., other series of conflicts had been followed between Sparta and Athens; Athens had suffered more defeats;
* In 404 B.C., Athens was forced by Sparta to sue for peace; the Athenian power was broken down.

From the above list of reviews, it is not difficult to see that the cause of war was more of a subjective matter than of an objective issue. After having enjoyed a certain period of peaceful growth, Athens became the most powerful empire among the Greek city-states. It was not forced by others to go to war. Obviously most of the conflicts had been initially launched by Athens, and for a number of occasions, it had broken the truce signed with other city-states.

Nye well assessed the cause of war between Sparta and Athens from three layers – the precipitating cause, the domestic situation and policies taken, and the external structure. While agreeing with some of his points, this analytical piece would intend to understand this issue from the subjective and objective perspectives, and also like to assume an alternative view that the subjective choice made by Athens had played a key role, compared to other number of factors including the domestic situation and the external environment, in leading to the eruption of war. In other words, the war, in the case between Sparta and Athens, was decided more by internal subjective choice than by external objective situation.

The subjectivity of the war firstly lied in the aggressive and imperial ambition of the Athenian empire as well as in the pride of the Athenians in their social system, which made Athens not fearful of taking adventures toward war. They believed that they were bound to prevail in the conflict with Spartans. As Nye wrote, "The Athenian mood was one of imperial greatness, with pride and patriotism about their city and their social system, and optimism about how they would prevail in the war."[5]

Secondly, the subjective nature of the conflict was also contributed by the leadership of Athens. Pericles, the Athenian emperor, favoured a war, and was mostly ready to take risks for war, as he believed that the war with Sparta was inevitable.

Thirdly, the subjectivity of the war can be illustrated by the fact that, even by the time when the external situation wasn't in Athens's advantage, it still didn't stop it taking further adventures against others. For instance, before the outbreak of the second Peloponnesian war, the balance of power structure among the Greek city-states seemed to have gradually turned into a challenging situation against Athens, mostly resulted by Athens's improper handling of its relations with other smaller city-states. They got irritated by Athens's aggressive policies, and some of them including Megara and Potidaea joined the Spartans' side after the war erupted. Unfortunately, even when the external situation wasn't in favour of Athens, instead of adjusting its position, it decided to take adventures.

Athens could have more choices apart from having gone to war. Nevertheless, it still had decided to take the most dangerous approach on a number of occasions. Therefore, the war was more of a matter subjectively chosen by Athens, than of an objective matter, under which, Athens was forced by the external balance of power structure to go to war.

There was a claim made by the Athenians to the Melians amid the Peloponnesian war that "the strong do what they have the power to do and the weak accept what they have to accept,"[6] which could probably have told the whole story behind the root cause of the Peloponnesian war.

"Prisoner's Dilemma", Two Prisoners, and Two States

Some especially those holding a realist proposition may tend to use the security dilemma faced by two prisoners to depict the difficult situation encountered by two states. This assessment would assume that this kind of analogy could be misleading to statesmen and policy-makers, and it is not appropriate to put such an analogy between the two groups given the different nature and characteristics between state actors and individuals.

In accordance with the "Prisoner's Dilemma" logic, the situation faced by two prisoners would only lead to a deadlock, and there would be no further way out for them. If statesmen are misguided by this type of logic, they would tend to believe in the inevitability of a conflict, and then a real war, as what had happened in history on a number of occasions, would most likely come to them. Once decision-makers believe in the inevitability of war, very likely they would give up their efforts to seek other means to solve the problem, and then the only major concern left to them should be the preparedness for war as well as the timing of war.

In reality, the dilemma faced by two prisoners, in contrast to the situation encountered by two states, should be much more difficult for the prisoners to overcome, if this issue can be analysed from a relative perspective.

The case for two individual prisoners is of a matter relating to domestic politics, while the relationship between two states is of an issue dealt with by international politics. In the domain of domestic politics, there is the law and government above the individuals, while in the arena of international politics, the international system is anarchy, there is no authoritarian government above the states. The difference remained between domestic politics and international politics in terms of their functions would directly lead to different results when thinking of the security dilemma faced by states and by individuals.

For the two individuals, they are certainly not allowed to challenge the law to negotiate with the police about the nature of the crime or about how many years they could possibly be staying in prison. These issues should be decided by the law. Besides that, there is a precondition that it is impossible for the two prisoners to communicate with each other in any means. Under these circumstances, the choices faced by them could include three possibilities: telling the truth to the police, lying, or keeping silent - telling the truth here also means prisoners' attempt to cheat on each other, since both of them generally don't trust that the other would stay in silence. Lying most likely cannot work, as it is impossible for the two prisoners, without any communication, to lie the same to the police. Staying silent is also unlikely, as already pointed, the two prisoners have basically no trust to each other. Thus, the only choice left for them is to tell the truth.

In the case of a security dilemma encountered by two states, international anarchy could be an important factor for having affected problem-solving among states, since under the anarchic system, states may perceive each other more from pessimistic perspectives and tend to be suspicious of others' intentions, as realists generally believed.

However, anarchy doesn't mean completely fragmentation and disorder. At both regional and international levels, besides states, there are international law, norms, rules and mechanisms, as well as a variety of transnational organizations, groups, and agencies having been joining in the process of improving the international system. With the growing role of this range of actors in regional and international affairs, the negative effects of anarchy have been relatively reduced. The anarchic international system with the participation of non-states actors has provided sates with alternative channels or platforms to handle the security dilemmas met by them.

Once two states are trapped in a security dilemma, they should have more choices than prisoners. They should have more freedoms and leeway to help get them out of the deadlock. For instance, one of the two states could choose to directly approach the other one through diplomatic or non-diplomatic channels; or they could get a third party involved to play a mediating role. Over all, the most noticeable advantage for states, in contrast to prisoners, in facing a security trap is that states can communicate with each other, and have the rights and capacity to negotiate in any ways as far as they would like to make an effort to do so.

In addition, individuals compared to states are in much more vulnerable positions in both physical and mental terms. For example, if one of the two states cheated on the other, another one could in response deploy a number of means – retaliating by playing "tit for tat" games, suing the issue to international law, getting a third party to mediate, or applying any other political and economic means. Apart from that, states can afford to make small mistakes in line with their capabilities. As far as they are able to correct the mistakes and shift their actions and policies to the right direction as quickly as they can, more severe consequences can be avoided, and resilience can be restored after all. However, the timing and chances for making further mistakes by prisoners, once they are taken into prison, should be very limited, unless they would want to bear more severe punishments.

Therefore, the security dilemma for two prisoners should be something which is very hard for them to surpass, while the security dilemma for two states should be an issue that can be handled and overcome by state actors. It is not appropriate to take the security dilemma encountered by states and by prisoners to a parallel position to understand. Statesmen and policy-makers should avoid being misled by the "Prisoner's Dilemma" logic.

Understanding the "Thucydides Trap" Argument in the New Era

This session is to examine how states could overcome the "Thucydides Trap" in today's world. This can be assessed from both the objective and subjective perspectives.

From the objective perspective, the world today is not the one that Thucydides had ever lived. When Thucydides wrote *History of the Peloponnesian War*, the author's thinking was constrained by history, geography, and technology, as well as by the political, economic, and social progresses made by humans over the past centuries more broadly. Besides that, in modern times, numerous changes and advancement in a wide variety of sectors have occurred, and they have set the preconditions to make states feel more difficult to go to war.

People living in Thucydides's days and even in the recent past centuries were no need to deal with non-security challenges such as climate change, natural disaster, pollution and so on, as faced by humans living in today's world. People and the societies by then were separated by borders and had limited interactions. There were no issues related to terrorism, drug trafficking, and other kind of trans-border crimes.

However, starting from the second half of last century, with the development of information technology, as well as with the invention of other series of advanced technologies in various industries, the world has gradually turned into a more globalized society. People and countries have never been as closely connected as they are today.

Nuclear weapons, international rules, norms, and mechanisms, the established regional and international organizations and institutions, and the growing participation of non-state actors in international affairs have played tremendous parts in restraining states from taking extreme actions under difficult situations.

From the subjective perspective, the issue of whether being able to avoid or overcome the security trap very much depends on the subjective thinking of and the actions taken by decision-makers. The most crucial issue for them is to avoid being further misguided by the "Prisoner's Dilemma" logic, as already suggested in the previous session of this analysis.

In retrospect of what had happened in history, in most cases wars had been subjectively chosen by states, rather than the other way around that states had been chosen by wars. There might be exceptional cases beyond such claim – A state could be forced into war. It decides to get into war because of being attacked in the first place, and going to war is acted as a matter of self-defence. If this is the case, the state is chosen by war.

The final point this analysis would like to make is that in case two states fail to surpass a security dilemma and a war between them is unleashed, states should avoid once again being dragged into the same logic by linking the war with the "Thucydides Trap" argument, as many experts and politicians did previously. There is a necessity for them to see that going to war is indicative of states having subjectively given up other means to get themselves out of the security dilemma. After all, it is still of a subjective and epistemological issue for policy-makers.

Conclusion

The first session of this piece, after having assessed the "Thucydides Trap" argument, reached a point that the security trap argument was inadequate in interpreting the root cause of war between Sparta and Athens, as it had obviously overestimated the role of the objective matter – the rising of Athens and the fear it caused in Sparta – in deciding the outbreak of the war, while having underestimated Athens's subjective choice in sparking the conflict. The second session on the "Prisoner's Dilemma" logic made a point that the security dilemma encountered by state actors and by prisoners cannot be put into a parallel position to understand, given the different nature and severity of the security situation faced by the two groups. Then a concluding point made by the second session was that the security trap can be very hard for prisoners to overcome, yet it could be surpassed by states. The final session re-affirmed the points made by the previous two sessions, as well as analysed how the series of objective and subjective factors in today's world have actually set higher conditions to prevent states from going to extreme.

The advancement of military technologies decides that the nature of wars in today's world is much more catastrophic than that in the previous centuries. Even a small scale conflict between two states could generate a disastrous impact on a great number of people and the societies they live. The issues of poverty, refugee crisis, disease transmission, and crimes, as well as other series of social, economic, and political problems in certain countries nowadays often cannot be separated from the series of small conflicts among relevant states. Thus, how to help state actors, in particular, the great powers, overcome the possible security traps in the future should be a crucial subject for statesmen, intellectuals, and practitioners to study.

Notes

1. Corcyra and Corinth were city-states in ancient Greece.

2. See Nye Joseph (2000). *Understanding International Conflicts: An Introduction to Theory and History* (Third Edition). PP.13. LONGMAN: An imprint of Addison Wesley Longman, Inc.

3. Ibid. PP.17. Also see Kagan Donald (1969). *The Outbreak of the Peloponnesian War.* NY: Cornell University Press.

4. Information related to the list of historical events having recorded the conflicts among the Greek city-states is from Nye, *Understanding International Conflicts.*

5. Ibid. PP.14.

6. See Nye, *Understanding International Conflicts.* Also see Thucydides (1972). *History of the Peloponnesian War.* PP.55. London: Penguin.

II. Liberal Values and the Liberal International Order: Limits and Future Direction

Professor Joseph Nye in 2017 ever wrote an article titled "American Leadership and the Future of the Liberal International Order."[1] In that article, he listed three possible challenges to a U.S.-led liberal international order - economic and financial capability, interventionism, and domestic political division. According to his observation, the real challenge to a U.S.-led liberal order among this three would be of domestic division. In other words, the real challenge to American leadership in a liberal world would come from the U.S. inside such as the domestic political division and the rise of populism, rather than from its outside like the threats from other powers.[2]

Given the strength of the U.S. power in a number of core areas including the economic, military, and technological aspects of the U.S. power as well as its soft power, Nye argued that a U.S.-led liberal international order would continue. Yet he also indicated that the liberal order could be altered in certain ways. One of the phenomena could be that, with the rise of other powers and the complexities this could cause, the U.S. would feel more difficult to organize actions. Another phenomenon under a new liberal order is that, with part of the power being transferred from states to non-state actors alongside the advancement of information technology, there could be more unfamiliar complexities for governments.[3]

While agreeing with the above assessment on the possible phenomena to appear under a new liberal order, this analytical piece would meanwhile focus on the exploration of values and of their impacts on a future liberal international order. To do so, it would assume a view that the values for driving changes and forging a future liberal order might be enriched and be more pluralistic alongside certain non - western values also with a liberal nature possibly gaining more influence on the global stage.

Among the number of challenging factors to the liberal international order, apart from what having been examined by other observers, this piece would assume that the way how the liberal values have been promoted has significantly affected some people's understanding and impression to the liberal values themselves, as well as to a U.S.-led liberal order; and these kinds of understanding and impression could still generate a challenging effect to the U.S. aspiration and effort in facilitating a new liberal order.

Over the past decades, the promotion of liberal values and of a liberal order has generally borne a purpose of serving the U.S. strategic interest. Yet in the process of doing so, numerous repercussions have also been arisen on both the domestic and international levels. This paper will begin by briefly analysing the origin of the liberal values; then it will assess the repercussions emerged in the process of promoting the liberal values; and finally, it will try to foresee how a future liberal international order might be like. The purpose of doing this analysis is to see whether there might be an alternative solution for states, in particular, the major powers, to jointly forge and sustain a new liberal international order.

On the Liberal Values

According to Professor Francis Fukuyama's narratives, classical liberalism emerged in the European continent in the late 17th and 18th centuries, and was created to serve as a solution to address religious conflicts, as well as to peacefully deal with problems raised in the pluralistic societies. Modern liberals like John Locke, instead of linking the liberal doctrine closely with politics or religion, sought to honour life itself and to take liberalism into a realm of mainly dealing with private matters. The interpretation to "life, liberty, and the pursuit of happiness" stipulated in the Declaration of Independence can be traced to this type of modern liberal tradition. Meanwhile, the liberal tradition in continental Europe had been developed toward an even deeper meaning, which not only served as a mechanism for managing conflicts, but also as a means for protecting "fundamental human dignity." [4]

Human dignity, in line with the Christian tradition, was "universally shared and made human beings equal in the sight of God."[5] By the Enlightenment age, "the capacity for choice or individual autonomy was given a secular form by thinkers like Rousseau ('perfectibility') and Kant (a 'good will'), and became the ground for the modern understanding of the fundamental right to dignity written into many 20th-century constitutions."[6]

From the above narratives, we can see that the evolution of the liberal doctrine is mostly closely connected to the west. Therefore, liberal values are usually perceived by many as western values. Nevertheless, in reality, numerous thoughts and values of being liberal in substantial terms are not solely western-related.

According to Fukuyama's observation, "the most fundamental principle enshrined in liberalism is one of tolerance."[7] Throughout the human history, a lot of values and thoughts - which also recognize the significance of inclusiveness or tolerance in managing diversities and differences in both private and public affairs - did not derive from or were created by the west. For instance, the Chinese value of "Harmony/ Coexistence but not Sameness/Uniformity" or of "A Community of Shared Future for Mankind" can be understood as such.

In this regard, from the conceptual or theoretical perspective, liberal values appear to have more relevance to the west, yet in substantial terms, liberal values should be connected to a wide variety of civilizations and cultures, even though there wasn't a concept of liberalism created by the non-western world back in the 17th and 18th centuries.

Linking liberalism with individual humans, liberal values recognize every human being's equal rights in freedom of belief, of expression, of association, and of assembly.

In terms of the liberal doctrine's relevance to domestic politics, some usually think that liberalism parallels with a democratic political system in a society. While according to Fukuyama's investigation, "liberalism is connected to democracy, but is not the same thing as it is".[8] A democratic regime may not be liberal - today's India can be considered as such; or a liberal regime may not be a democracy - Germany in the 19th century belonged to this category. [9]

With regard to liberal values' connection to international politics, the promotion of liberal values is mostly related to globalization and the forging and sustaining of a liberal international order, under which, numerous international governmental and non-governmental organizations, transnational corporations, and other range of transnational actors join their forces together with state actors to promote regionalism, multilateralism, and international cooperation etc.

From a conceptual perspective, liberal values weigh liberty and equality, and uphold a principle of inclusiveness or tolerance. Yet, the practice of liberalism in many occasions appears to have gone to a different direction especially in a way by having neglected other range of values. This kind of neglect has caused numerous repercussions in both the domestic and international dimensions.

Repercussions Arisen in the Process of Practising the Liberal Values

On the domestic level of some democracies, the voices of safeguarding the liberal values such as voices of defending human rights and of opposing discrimination are usually high. Yet various forms of discrimination have always been an issue in these societies. Why has discrimination always been an issue? There is a dilemma here over this issue - on the one hand, in conceptual terms, liberal values hold a principle that every human being is born equal; on the other hand, some practitioners of the liberal values have somehow sought to take this doctrine exclusive.

Fukuyama made a more systemic argument over the criticisms made to liberalism from both the left and the right of the American liberal society, including the issue of discrimination. According to his observation, the right accused liberal values of having undermined the national identity, as well as the shared values and culture of a particular community; while the left critics pointed that equality empowered by the law does not mean equality in real life, as reflected by the fact that discrimination and other forms of injustices appear frequently in the liberal societies; and "those injustices have become identities around which people could mobilize."[10] Though there are differences between the right and the left in terms of their criticisms to liberalism, generally, they do have a structural similarity over this issue – which is that "liberal society does not do enough to root out deep-seated racism, sexism, and other forms of discrimination, so politics must go beyond liberalism".[11] After all, discrimination in certain liberal societies is of a systemic issue, as many have already indicated.

In addition to the above, the promotion of liberal values has generated big social, economic, and cultural impacts on some group of people. It has also affected significantly of domestic politics in certain ways. Discrimination and the rise of populism cannot be separated from this. The following part will discuss the various impacts in more details.

From the economic perspective, the liberal doctrine appears to have overvalued the market role in handling economic and financial activities. Observers generally believed that the 2008 financial crises were caused by deregulation and lack of proper state intervention in core financial and economic activities.

While certain countries believing in the efficiency of a full market-driven economy, China has developed a different model, which allows both the state and the market to have a play in economic activities, and let the Chinese market open progressively. Due to the application of a slow and incremental approach, China had avoided being hit as hardly as its developed counterparts had during the 2008 financial crisis.

By drawing on the lessons from the Asian financial

crises, the 2008 global financial crises, and other series of repercussions generated by deregulation, as well as by taking into account a broader context of the domestic and international situations in the post-pandemic era, states will have to rethink about how to make a proper balance between the market role and government intervention in economic activities.

In the case of China, to accommodate the changing domestic and international environments, China has released a dual circulation economic policy, which basically means that, while continuingly being committed to opening-up, China would prioritize its domestic circulation and meet its domestic demands, and in the meantime, seek to make domestic and international dual circulations reinforce each other. This dual circulation pattern can be a most recent example to show how Chinese government attempted to seek a balance between domestic market and international market through policy intervention in order to alleviate the possible repercussions and damages in the post- COVID-19 pandemic period.

Another issue concerning the economic consequences caused by promoting liberal values is of inequality. Alongside the globalization process, the uncontrolled and fast liberalization and privatization of certain industries in some developing and developed countries during the 1980s and 1990s had led to the huge and fast accumulation of resources, capital, and profits by large corporations, powerful individuals, and other forms of big sectors, as a result of that process, inequality and the gap between the rich and the poor had become major concerns for policy-makers. China, like many other countries, also had to face the inequality challenge.

Apparently, the repercussions led by globalization and liberalization have not only significantly affected developed countries but also developing ones. Thus, when globalization and liberalization are entering a new stage now, the issue of how to promote a more inclusive and balanced growth and make the growth benefit as more people as possible should become one of the primary concerns for world leaders. In recent few years, we have seen a worldwide rising of populism. The inequality factor should be one of the main contributors to it.

From the social and cultural perspectives, the consequences of promoting liberal values are closely connected to the economic impact of doing that, which has led to the declining social status of certain group of people especially in the western societies. Apart from that, immigration also has made a great number of people feel that their shared tradition, values, and culture have been threatened, and as a consequence, many have faced an identity crisis. After all, the social and cultural impact of promoting liberal values is also of a key contributor to populism and domestic divisions.

Furthermore, from the political aspect, the alliance of liberal values and the democratic system is designed to facilitate a platform for major political parties, based on debates and discussions, to secure consensus on issues concerning the countries' core interests. Nevertheless, very often the intensive debates and discussions, instead of securing or implementing consensus, have led to more delays and more divisions among the parties. In the case of the United States, being unable to agree on certain measures and policies timely as well as not being able to enforce properly of the secured measures have caused a series of delays in addressing the COVID-19. Now, concerning the election, though the election is over, it is not certain what is going to happen for some time to come. Divisions among the political parties and among the people could be difficult issues for the United States to deal with in a long term.

Overall, from the above analysis, we can see that the promotion of liberal values has generated big economic, social, cultural, and political impacts on various societies of the world. The negative repercussions have led to divisions and the rise of populism, which in turn have posed a threat to the current liberal international order.

In the case of the U.S., Nye argued that the rising populistic politics could be a major threat to a U.S.-led liberal international order in the future, as the populistic politics could affect the U.S. readiness to lead on a number of issues such as climate change.[12]

In response to the challenges led by the rise of populism, the U.S. government has taken a series of measures including tightening border control and the immigration policies, encouraging the U.S. companies to move back to the U.S., waging trade wars against foreign countries, and limiting transnational communications and exchanges in various ways.

However, given the close interconnection and interdependence of different parts of the world facilitated by the advancement of technologies, it is hard to believe that a protectionist approach could work out well to help address the populists' movement. To properly manage the dilemma between the rising populism and the continuing promotion of liberal values, more targeted domestic economic policies and measures to meet the concerns of populists may need to take into account. Apart from that, enhancing governance capacity at all levels of governments and promoting social cohesion, inclusiveness, and unity among the people and groups coming from a wide variety of racial and cultural backgrounds should also be advisable from a long-term perspective.

The final point concerning the impact of the liberal doctrine is of legitimacy - more precisely, the legitimacy of the liberal international order driven by liberal values. Many observers already questioned the legitimacy of a liberal international order, and argued that it lacks a broad legitimacy on the global level. The U.S. strategist Dr. Henry Kissinger ever pointed that "No truly global 'world order' has ever existed. What passes for order in our time was devised in Western Europe nearly four centuries ago, at a peace conference in the German region of Westphalia, conducted without the involvement or even the awareness of most other continents or civilizations." [13]

After WWII, the international system for a certain period of time had been divided into two major camps - the socialist camp and the capitalist camp, respectively led by the former Soviet Union and the United States. The two camps had had limited economic and business engagements. A post-war economic order was established under the U.S. leadership. Within the capitalist camp, certain core liberal values had so far been only shared by the U.S. and its key allies. From the 1980s on till the end of the Cold War, with the globalization process speeding up, the influence of liberal values had further been expanded. Then after the Cold War, they have obtained a series of new momentums on the global stage in terms of driving globalization and liberalization.

The problem is that, while some may have benefited from the current liberal order, the liberal values and liberal order have also generated a lot of obstacles for a large number of countries, in particular, the developing nations, because they don't always fit well the domestic conditions of those countries. Very often the values and the system cannot solve the fundamental problems faced by a lot of them. For example, many African countries are democracies. However, for decades already, the liberal values and the democratic system haven't so far helped address their problems properly such as poverty, governance, health, and so on.

Nonetheless, it may not be appropriate to argue that all the problems just assessed above lie in the liberal values themselves. A lot of problems should also lie in the practice of liberal values. As for some developing countries, applying liberal values without having taken their domestic conditions into enough consideration could be one of the key reasons for having not made big improvement in a number of core areas. Therefore, selectively applying the principles of the liberal values as well as of other range of values in dealing with specific matters under different circumstances is more advisable.

Overall, quite a lot of repercussions have arisen in the process of promoting liberal values and of sustaining a liberal international order over the past years. By drawing the lessons accumulated in the past, what could a future liberal international order be like?

A Future Liberal International Order

The world would possibly develop toward a direction with more complexities and uncertainties. To forge a sound liberal international order, and avoid the world turning into isolationism or going back to a period like the first half of the 20th century, which was occupied by devastating conflicts and casualties, major powers and influential international organizations will be expected to continue to play significant roles in terms of creating public goods while allowing more freedom, inclusiveness, and flexibility in regional and international cooperation. For instance, in the U.S. position, in Nye's words, to sustain an American liberal order, "it will not be enough to think in terms of

American power over others. One must also think in terms of power to accomplish joint goals which involve power with others."[14]

Meanwhile, this analysis would share a view that two key phenomena might appear alongside the process of forging a new liberal order.

First, the value system to facilitate a new liberal order would be enriched and be more pluralistic with non-western liberal values possibly acquiring more spaces in the value system.

Only by including the range of values from different cultural backgrounds into the value system, applying alternatively the sound and positive aspects of various values, abandoning the shortcomings and negative aspects of certain values, and seeking commonalities among a variety of values, conflicting interests among major powers as well as among different races and cultures can be avoided or minimized, to that extent, a sound liberal international order can be shaped and sustained.

In the Chinese society, a number of great thinkers in history had ever subsequently produced various schools of thoughts such as Confucianism, Taoism, and others etc. Buddhism was also introduced to China in ancient times and being incorporated into the Chinese tradition. Unlike the religious wars having ever happened in the west, there have never been any real conflicts among the variety of thoughts and religions in the Chinese society. In different periods of the long Chinese history, there had usually been a dominant thought mixed with other schools of thoughts to jointly formulate part of the Chinese tradition and influence the Chinese society. In a simplest way, this kind of value tradition can be described as "Unity with Plurality". In contrast, though liberalism also upholds a key principle of tolerance in order to deal with differences in a pluralistic society, yet the practice of this principle has gone to a opposite direction in many occasions.

Anyway, the Chinese experiences in managing the relationship among various schools of thoughts proved that there are no fundamental conflicts among the good aspects of all range of values - western, eastern, or others; and there should be a great deal of commonalities among them. As far as the principle of inclusiveness and of coexistence among them can be applied substantially at the international stage, a peaceful liberal international order can be sustained.

On the same issue, Dr. Kissinger put a more strategic view. He argued that:

"World order cannot be achieved by any one country

acting along. To achieve a genuine world order, its components, while maintaining their own values, need to acquire a second culture that is global, structural, and juridical - a concept of order that transcends the perspective and ideals of any one region or nation. At this moment in history, this would be a modernization of the Westphalian system informed by contemporary realities."[15]

Second, with part of the power being shifted away from states to non-state actors, influential international organizations like the United Nations and others will be expected to play more crucial roles in terms of helping forge and sustain a new liberal order, especially with regard to the aspects of promoting the inclusiveness of the relevant range of values and ideologies, as well as of helping secure more flexibility and fairness in international cooperation.

Conclusion

In a world full of uncertainties, how the major powers like the U.S. and China engage with each other would significantly affect the nature and direction of a future liberal international order. There is a necessity for the major powers to look at each other differently from the way how great powers in history had look at and dealt with each other.

Regarding the future of the liberal international order, China has expressed support to an UN-centred international system as well as a world order based on international law, given that the UN memberships represent the interests of a majority of the international community, rather than that of a small circle of countries.

Regardless of whether the future liberal order will be U.S.-led, or jointly led by the major powers with greater participation of international organizations and other range of non-state actors, in order to avoid conflicts and to sustain a sound order, world leaders may have to accept the multi-polarization of values in the process of shaping a new global order. They also have to see that creating and sustaining a new liberal order needs a great deal of careful calculation - calculation of internal and external environments, of the balance between freedom and order, of the legitimacy and justice of order and so on - in Dr. Kissinger's words, "order must be cultivated; it cannot be imposed." [16] Similarly, neither can values be imposed.

Notes

1. Nye Joseph (2018). "American Leadership and the

Future of the Liberal International Order". *China International Strategy Review 2018.* PP. 1-15

2. Ibid.

3. Ibid.

4. Fukuyama Francis (2020). "Liberalism and Its Discontents: the Challenges from the Left and the Right". *American Purpose.* 5 October 2020. https://www.americanpurpose.com/articles/liberalism -and-its-discontent/

5. Ibid.

6. Ibid.

7. Ibid.

8. Ibid.

9. Ibid.

10. Ibid.

11. Ibid.

12. See Nye, "American Leadership and the Future of the Liberal International Order".

13. Quoted in Kissinger Henry (2015). *World Order.* Penguin Books. PP.2-3

14. See Nye, "American Leadership and the Future of the Liberal International Order".

15. See Kissinger, *World Order.* PP.373

16. In the context of Kissinger's writing, the sentence of "order must be cultivated; it cannot be imposed." was used to make an argument on the appropriate

balance between order and freedom. The author of this piece views that it also fits the context of this analysis well when it was used to highlight the significance of careful calculation and cultivation in the process of forging and sustaining a sound liberal order.

Chapter 2

Major Power Relations, Global Governance, and World Order

I. Global Governance Is at A New Cross Road

Global governance has reached a new cross road since the world moved into the new century. A series of mechanisms and institutions within the global governance system have lost part of their efficiency; meanwhile a set of new mechanisms established since the beginning of the new century somehow haven't got institutionalized and functioned well yet. The number of issues faced by the world today urged nations to make efforts to improve the system in order to better address the challenges under the new situation. Nevertheless, countries especially the big powers so far haven't been able to reach a common understanding in general terms on what approach should be adopted to improve the current system. It appears that the world only super power, the United States, is in favour of a conventional approach, which basically means that the U.S. still plays a major role in global rule-making, while other countries across the globe are mostly in a position of being the rule-takers; or we can also assume that the U.S. may just need a bit longer time to finally recognize that a fairer and more balanced global governance approach, rather than a traditional approach, should be more suitable to both the U.S. and other countries.

In the meantime, some developing countries and emerging economies, as well as those smaller developed countries with great potential and strength in special issue areas would prefer to have fairer and more balanced participation in regional and global affairs.

Some developing countries and smaller industrialized nations have been making efforts to promote the democratization of international relations for decades already. Certain progresses have been made. The establishment of the Group of Twenty (G20) mechanism can be a good example to represent a big progress of the global governance system. Through the G20 mechanism, developing and developed countries finally stand together to deal with common challenges in the global economic and financial area.

More progress in promoting the democratization of international relations in the coming years needs to be made, given that the world has been changing and the changes in a wide range of issue areas require an increasing and more balanced participation from both developing and developed states as well as from the non-state actors in terms of their contributions to regional and global governance.

Though there could be numerous factors - such as

problems existed in certain international organizations or other various transnational actors - that have affected the improvement of the global governance system. Instead of focusing on the exploration of all kinds of factors in great details, this analysis would aim to, from a broader and structural perspective, assess the impacts of state actors, in particular, of the major powers on the global governance system. In other words, it would attempt to observe how the various approaches - an unilateral and hegemonic approach or a fairer and more cooperative approach - taken by the major powers have affected and would continue to significantly affect the global efforts in improving the global governance system. To do that, it would assume a view that a hegemonic approach taken by the U.S., instead of contributing to global governance, should be one of the main causes for having slowed down the process of improving global governance. Then, this analytical piece will suggest a possible solution for overcoming the issues that have constrained the cooperation among major powers. Before doing all that, it will firstly give a brief historical overview of the development of global governance since the end of WWII.

A Brief Historical Overview of Global Governance

Global governance has roughly experienced three

periods since the end of WWII: from 1945 to the 1970s, from the 1970s to the late 20th century, and from the end of the 20th century to present.

From 1945 to the 1970s, though the concept of "Global Governance" wasn't created yet, states, as the main actors in international relations, plus a number of international institutions consisting of the International Monetary Fund, the World Bank, and the United Nations as well as various others had already been in main positions of practicing global governance. By then, inter-state relations and inter-governmental relations had mattered a lot in terms of their relevance to regional and global affairs.

Under the leadership of the victorious nations, particularly, of the United States, a post-war world order was forged, as reflected by the establishment of the United Nations as well as of the Bretton Woods Institutions mainly consisting of the General Agreement on Tariffs and Trade (the World Trade Organization) the International Monetary Fund, and the International Bank for Reconstruction and Development (the World Bank).

Over this period, many developing countries had just achieved national independence. Domestic construction and recovery had become the priorities of these countries. Generally, developing countries had had limited participation in global governance and international cooperation.

From the security, geopolitical, and ideological perspectives at the international stage, the U.S.-led capitalist camp and the former Soviet Union-led socialist camp had competed for dominance. Ideologies had mattered a lot in terms of affecting the relationship and cooperation among nation states. The developing world and the developed world generally had secured limited collaboration, coordination and communication.

For supporting its Cold War policy, the U.S. started to implement the Marshall Plan shortly after WWII to help recover the European economy, which in turn strengthened the power and influence of the U.S.-led capitalist camp. During the 1960s-1970s, the U.S. had suffered a series of difficulties in both domestic and international dimensions, along with the oil crises, the dollar crises, the uncontrolled movement of financial capital across borders, as well as the U.S.-Vietnam war etc. Nevertheless, it had finally managed to overcome the series of challenges and further made a lot of achievements, particularly, in the economic field, as indicated by the formation of an economic model driven by a neo-liberal school of thought. Besides that, in the mid-1970s, the major developed countries established the Group of Seven (G7) mechanism, which served as one of the few main platforms for dealing with global political and economic issues.

Overall, during the post-war years, the U.S.-led major developed countries had been in a key position in leading the direction of global governance and international collaboration. By then the GDP of the G7 member countries accounted for around 70% of the global total, and the trade volume over 50%.[1]

The second period of global governance was ranging from the 1970s to the late 20th century. A number of important events had taken place at the international stage over this period - the world turned from bipolar to unipolar with the dissolution of the former Soviet Union; China and the U.S. formalized their diplomatic relations in 1979; China adopted a reform and opening-up policy starting from 1978, and later from the mid-1990s gradually developed a socialist market economy.

Globalization was deepened, and it had greatly influenced the developing and developed worlds in both negative and positive ways.

The negative implications of globalization roughly manifested from the following aspects: it had generated uncertainties and vulnerabilities. Developing and less-developed regions and countries, as well as the small businesses in different countries could have suffered more from these uncertainties and vulnerabilities, due to the fact that, these less-developed regions and countries in the early stage of globalization generally had lacked advanced technologies, capital, and governance capacity to help them endure the consequences of globalization. Also, the global businesses run by big transnational corporations, compared to the small businesses, were more competitive and obviously in more advantageous positions to benefit from globalization. Therefore, globalization somehow had created inequalities and widened the gap between the rich and the poor.

In the meantime, globalization had also created positive outcomes. Countries from different parts of the world had been more closely connected over this period. A large number of developing and less-developed countries, as well as a great deal of small businesses from different regions had got on to the regional and international level-playing fields and gradually grown stronger. The period from the 1970s to the late 20th century had also been of a very significant time for countries, both developing and developed, to re-adjust their positions and policies. The developing and developed worlds had been more closely integrated and inter-connected with each other.

In addition, apart from state actors, the emergence of a wide variety of non-state actors including the set of mechanisms in different areas had promoted globalization and global governance up to a new stage. Apparently, the type of participants in contributing to global governance and problem-solving had been greatly widened. Though ideology was still of an issue, it had played a much less crucial role in affecting the relationship and cooperation among various actors.

Alongside a great deal of dramatic changes at the global stage, the concept of "Global Governance" was formulated. The former West German Chancellor Willy Brandt and the then Swedish Prime Minister Ingvar Carlsson had greatly contributed to the process of forging this concept. As initially proposed by the then West German Chancellor in early 1990s that the world needed a new concept to handle the uncertainties and challenges in a more globalized world after the Cold War, and then after having gone through a series of discussions in international summits, the concept named "Global Governance" firstly appeared in a report titled "Our Global Neighbourhood", which was released by the Commission on Global Governance. Soon this new concept of "Global Governance" was widely recognized and applied at the global stage.[2]

Overall, the first and second periods of global governance had proved the U.S. confidence in ascertaining its leadership in rule-making and network-building. Meanwhile, the second stage of global governance had also exhibited the strength and potential of certain developing countries and small industrialized nations in terms of their engagements in global affairs.

From the late 20th century to present, a series of events including the 1997 Asian financial crises, China's entry into the WTO, the 9.11 terrorist attacks, and the 2008 global financial crises, as well as the current coronavirus pandemic etc. have had big impacts on the global political and economic landscapes. Dramatic progress has taken place in the global governance sphere, along with the growing role of developing countries and emerging economies in global affairs, as well as with the springing up of a number of new mechanisms and organizations such as the Shanghai Cooperation Organization (SCO), the G20, the BRICS, the Asian Infrastructure and Investment Bank (AIIB), and so on.

To better deal with the repercussions of the Asian financial crises, as well as to avoid further crises to happen, the G20 summit, as proposed by the Finance Ministers of the Group of Eight countries, was formed on 16 December 1999 in Berlin. Then years later in order to help rescue the developed world out of the 2008 global financial crises, the G20 summit was upgraded to the leader's level in 2008. Soon in 2009, the G20 replaced the G7 to become the primary international platform for managing global economic and financial affairs. The establishment of the G20 marked a big progress for the improvement of the global governance system.

A Unilateral and Hegemonic Approach - One of the Main Causes for Having Affected the Improvement of the Global Governance System

In retrospect, the U.S.-led major developed nations had been able to independently deal with their own problems in the past century. By then, developing and less developed countries had been in relative weak positions and they had played a minor role in global governance. Nevertheless, different parts of the world nowadays are more closely connected. The contribution of developing countries to the world has kept growing while the role of developed countries has diminished a bit. The management of the 2008 global financial crises as well as of the current pandemic proved that certain developed countries are not capable of independently handling the series of crises anymore. They need a wider participation of various actors. Therefore, the new situation needs a new global governance approach. The new approach basically means that developing and developed countries and other range of actors need to work together to promote the improvement of the global governance system in a pragmatic way. This should be a general trend of global governance in the 21st century.

However, certain U.S. politicians and policy advisers don't seem to be ready to support this new approach at the moment. Rather they would still prefer a traditional approach - mainly a U.S.- led unilateral and hegemonic approach - which is supposed to meet the U.S. interest in the first place, while a large number of others bearing more international responsibilities without being able to enjoy the rights they are supposed to have. With the U.S. new administration taking office, it is not certain in what way the new government would tend to promote global governance and forge global rule-making; and further whether certain means to be taken by the new administration would work out well, given that the coronavirus pandemic has already altered both the U.S. and the world dramatically.

In reality, instead of contributing to the global governance system, a traditional approach, under the new circumstances, appears to have constrained the improvement of the whole system on the one hand; And on the other hand, the U.S. itself cannot benefit any longer from promoting a traditional approach, as by doing so, the U.S. might risk isolating itself from others. The traditional approach could lead to a possibility that a group of countries including developing countries, emerging economies, and less powerful developed countries might come together to form new mechanisms and rules in accordance with their common interests on certain areas of issues. The world has already seen this trend, as illustrated by the formation of a series of new institutions and platforms since the beginning of the new century.

Generally, from the above analysis, we can see that global governance has reached a new cross road now. To surpass the challenges at this cross road, this piece would finally put the following:

Sound and effective coordination and collaboration among major powers should still be very significant for the world to overcome the numerous challenges in the global governance sphere. In today's world, a unilateral and hegemonic approach most likely cannot work anymore. Rules have to be made based on the consideration of fairness and equality, rather than of the interests of one or of a few major powers. A fairer and more balanced global governance system means more opportunities for all, and it is conducive to the U.S. interest in remaining as the most powerful country in the world.

Notes

1. See He Yafei (2015). *China's Historical Choice in Global Governance.* Renmin University Press. PP.17

2. Ibid. PP.2-3

II. Prospects of China-U.S. Bilateral Engagements in the Future

The U.S. election is over. Yet the impact of it will likely last for some time to come. On the domestic level, hailing domestic divisions will be a major concern for the next U.S. administration. In the international dimension, restoring trust, and building confidence and credibility will be a main focus of the next government. More precisely, for a relatively long time, the new U.S. government domestically will concentrate on improving governance capacity, promoting social cohesion, curing the divisions among the people, and thinking about how to make the U.S. system work better. Internationally, it will make efforts to restore the U.S. leadership and reputation, and recover the U.S. relations with its allies.

Another key priority on the global level for the next administration would be to re-adjust the U.S. policies concerning the great power relations. Given the significance of China-U.S. relations to the two countries and the world, as well as that the U.S. has categorized China as one of its main competitors, China-U.S. bilateral ties will continue to be on the high agenda of the next government.

Yet, the next administration, instead of copying the Trump government's approach in dealing with China, will likely try to seek new ways to engage with China, with an objective of guaranteeing the U.S. interests on the one hand, and of avoiding conflicts between the two great powers on the other hand.

This study aims to assess the prospects of China-U.S. bilateral cooperation and competition from the following core areas: foreign and security issues, economy and trade, technology, and global governance.

Foreign and Security Policy

With the world moving into the 21 Century, a series of incidents happened during the first decade of the new century including the 9.11 terrorist attack and the 2008 global financial crises had caused serious disruptions to the U.S. usual policy agenda. In response to the terrorist attacks and other series of crises in the Middle East, the U.S. had subsequently taken a range of moves including launching a "War on Terror" strategy, sending troops to Afghanistan, and invading Iraq etc. Nevertheless, the U.S. involvement in the Middle East didn't make the situation there improve. Meanwhile in Europe, the European countries, like the United States, were by then troubled by the economic downturn led by the global financial crises.

Given the looming situation in the Middle East, as well as the economic difficulties encountered by the U.S. and its European counterparts dragged by the financial crises, in contrast to the relatively vibrant Asian region which suffered less from the financial crises, in order to get the U.S. out of the crises and further better serve the U.S. interests in a longer term, a "Return to Asia" strategy was put on the U.S. policy agenda by the Obama administration. The general objective of the "Return to Asia" strategy was designed to project and sustain the U.S. power and meet the best interests of the United States from both economic and security perspectives through working with its key allies as well as with the core regional organizations and institutions in Asia on the one hand; and to restrain China's influence and interests in this region on the other hand.

In Southeast Asia, because of the U.S. taking sides in the territorial disputes between China and its neighbours, for a period of time, China's relations with the Philippines and Vietnam had encountered certain challenges. Meanwhile, in East Asia, the U.S. had made attempts to press the Terminal High Altitude Area Defence (THAAD) system to be installed in South Korea, even though this move was strongly opposed by the South Korean locals.

Apparently, the U.S. had intended to act as a

balancer in the Asian region. However, losing impartiality and taking sides in the process of managing Asian regional affairs made the U.S. lose its legitimacy as a good balancer. By that period of time, its balance and involvement had only generated troubles and tensions, and resulted in more disruptions to regional peace and stability in many occasions.

In response to the U.S. "Rebalance of Asia" strategy, on the side of China and its Southeast Asian neighbours, under the joint efforts of relevant parties concerned, regional tension had been gradually eased. Further a Code of Conduct aiming to reconcile the differences of relevant parties and promote the settlement of regional disputes has been put on the negotiating table. Due to the concerted efforts, China's relationship with its Southeast Asian neighbours has step by step got back on track.

Around the same period of time in East Asia, because of the installation of the THAAD system as well as of other series of issues, the then South Korean president lost much of her popularity among the South Korean people, and finally was removed from the office. With president Moon taking office, China's relationship with South Korea has got improved further.

Overall, the easing of tension in Southeast Asia and East Asia and the improvement of China's relations with its neighbours symbolized the failure of the U.S. attempts to contain China through its "Return to Asia" strategy.

After Trump took office, the Trump administration announced an "Indo-pacific" strategy, which replaced the Obama government's "Rebalance of Asia" policy. Even though they are two different names, the general goal of this two is much the same. That is to maintain the U.S. influence in the Indo-pacific region from a security perspective, as well as to make the U.S. economically benefit from Asia's development. A minor difference between the two strategies might be that India could have been expected to play a more crucial role in accommodating the U.S. "Indo-pacific" strategy in terms of dealing with China.

The Trump government, compared to the Obama administration, has generally mainly focused on the U.S. economic gains, and also using the economic means to seek leverage over other areas of issues. Therefore, the Trump administration appears to have spent much less resources, in particular from a security sense, in implementing the U.S. "Indo-pacific" strategy. During the process of conducting this strategy, though the U.S. side occasionally had ever claimed its intention to work more closely with its allies and partners in Southeast Asia, so far no much clear and positive response from the relevant actors in this region had been unveiled.

Another character of the Trump government in handling China-U.S. competition on various core issues is that, instead of deploying the card of alliance relationship, the Trump administration has chosen to frequently play China's sovereign cards mainly consisting of issues related to Taiwan, Hong Kong, Tibet, and Xinjiang, as well as the economic card and the card of technology to pursue the U.S. interests - despite that the U.S. itself has suffered from the repercussions of those measures.

For instance, on the issue of Taiwan, apart from the arms sales to Taiwan, which were usually done by the previous U.S. administrations, the Trump government has taken a series of different moves - for instance, it has passed the "Taiwan Travel Act" in March 2018 and then the "Taipei Act" in March 2020, with the purpose of raising the stake in bargaining with China on economic gains.

In the meantime, Hong Kong, Xinjiang, and Tibet have been used to balance the U.S. foreign policy interests. The relevant accusations of China on human rights abuses in these regions from certain perspectives have been served as propaganda to undermine China's international image and soft power on the one hand, and as a leverage to meet the U.S.

economic bargaining interests on the other hand.

Then now with Biden being elected as the next U.S. president, what would be the policy agenda of the next U.S. administration concerning foreign and security issues? Would it return to the U.S. traditional way of dealing with China?

Some speculations have come up that the Biden administration's approach will be very much like Obama's. Some even called that as Obama's third term. In response, Biden himself has denied that. Meanwhile, he has declared that the U.S. is back and ready to reclaim leadership, and that the U.S. will seek to work more closely with its allies to handle common challenges.

Given the failures encountered by the previous administrations in dealing with China, plus the fact that the internal and external environments faced by the U.S. have changed dramatically compared to that years ago.

After taking office, one of the key priorities for the Biden Administration will be to restore the U.S. relationship with its core allies, particularly, its European allies, as many believed. In the meantime, the U.S. will attempt to seek alternative ways to interact with China. What the trilateral relationship of the U.S., China, and Europe could be like will be a big issue in modern international relations in the future.

In this trilateral relationship, even though the next U.S. administration might apply part of Obama's approach such as investing more efforts and resources in enhancing relationships with its European partners, the U.S. officials will likely think more carefully of the purpose of this relationship - for example, what the alliance relationship would be able to achieve? What benefits the U.S. can get from that alliance relationship from both the short term and long-term perspectives? How much resources the U.S. needs to invest for managing the existing conflicting interests with its European counterparts in both the economic and security aspects? Whether the cost of it would be larger than the benefits the U.S. can actually get? At the same time, on the side of the European countries, they would think the same questions as well, as the COVID-19 pandemic has caused a lot of changes, and in the post-pandemic era, countries would tend to pursue more pragmatic goals.

Anyway, in the immediate future, the U.S. next government will concentrate on dealing with a range of domestic issues in particular the COVID-19 pandemic and domestic divisions, which will slow down the process of the U.S. readiness to lead on certain other issues.

In an interview to the U.S. former Secretary of State Dr. Henry Kissinger in November by the

Bloomberg Editor-in-Chief upon an online convening of the New Economy Forum 2020, Dr. Kissinger, on China-U.S. bilateral ties, advised that the U.S. side needs to have dialogues with the Chinese leadership. The two countries can jointly agree on a structural framework, under which, they designate special high-level officials trusted by and representing the top leaders of both countries to regularly consult and communicate concerning some of the core issues in order to better understand each other. They need to explore and agree on what must be prevented - such as whatever kinds of disputes take place in other range of areas, a military conflict between the two powers will not happen; and then they can discuss what common goals can be reached. In addition to that, concerning certain disputes like issues related to human rights, both sides need to understand each other's sensitive points. They don't have to solve the problems immediately, yet at least they should make efforts to lower the seriousness of certain issues to a level that would allow both sides to have a leeway for further discussion.[1]

After all, managing the China-U.S. ties in the foreign and security aspect should be very sophisticated. Both sides will have to explore new alternative means in order to avoid being dragged into an uncontrollable situation.

Economy and Trade

After having gone through a few rounds of ups and downs over the past 70 years, China-U.S. bilateral economic and trade relations has developed from complete isolation during the 1950s-1960s to close inter-dependence and inter-connection at the present stage. Figures and facts can tell that both countries have greatly benefited from their economic and trade engagements. China-U.S. bilateral trade surpassed 630 billion USD in 2018.[2] The China-U.S. sound bilateral economic and trade relations has not only served as a stabilizer to the overall bilateral ties of the two countries, but also generated more certainties to the global economy as a whole.

Nevertheless, this relative stable economic relationship has undergone a series of disruptions since 2018 due to a trade war unilaterally launched by the U.S.. To implement the trade war policy, the U.S. has subsequently taken certain moves against China ranging from instigating 301 Investigation to imposing tariffs on Chinese products, and to sanctioning Chinese entities etc.

The U.S. side claimed that the purpose of the trade war was for managing the unbalanced trade between China and the United States - The U.S. has a large trade deficit with China in goods, because, over the years, China has taken advantage of the U.S.; China has caused the job losses in the U.S.; China is a currency manipulator; the U.S. companies have been forced to transfer their high technologies to Chinese companies and so on. These are the usual claims made by some U.S. officials. In reality, China hasn't taken advantage of the U.S. It should be the other way around. So, what is this trade deficit issue about?

The U.S. has a trade deficit with China in goods, while having a surplus in service trade. For the commodities manufactured in China, a large proportion of them have close linkages with the U.S. transnational corporations - either those amount of goods were produced by the joint ventures of American and Chinese manufacturing companies, or by the U.S. independently owned or invested companies; or the U.S. transnational corporations and investors may have other kinds of engagements in the designing, manufacturing, and selling processes of various goods.

Once the manufacturing process of the relevant products is completed, a proportion of them would go to the foreign markets, and in the meantime, a large amount of them would stay in the Chinese domestic market and be absorbed by the Chinese consumers. China's large market advantage plus its advantage in labour force have helped lower the production and shipping costs, and made the American businesses' investments in China more profitable generally, compared to their same amount of investments back in the U.S.

This whole process of marketing, designing, manufacturing, selling, and so on rightly reflects how the U.S.-advocated free market economic pattern works - the distribution of all relevant resources is driven by market demands and supplies. China hasn't taken advantage of the U.S. from this process. We can only say that a huge number of Chinese workers in the manufacturing industry, over the past decades, have been paid less and made more efforts and sacrifices than the manufacturing workers in the U.S..

In addition to that, the U.S. trade deficits with other countries including China were partly caused by its domestic structure problem. The shortcomings existed in the U.S. economic structure have led to its own losses. One of the examples is that the U.S. limits of its exports of high-end products to China have been a contributing factor for its deficit with China.

Two possible means can be applied to deal with the deficit issue with China - either the U.S. eases part of its export restrictive measures, or it pushes China to buy more U.S. products. As far as part of the U.S. export restrictive measures cannot be softened, further narrowing the deficit down to a level to make it meet the U.S. interests also means that China may risk buying certain American products that China doesn't really need. In other words, China has been pressed to bear part of the costs and losses generated by the U.S. domestic economic structure problems.

Given that finding a solution to address its domestic economic structure problem shouldn't be easy, launching a trade war and imposing tariffs on Chinese products seem to be the easier and more convenient measures, from the U.S. perspective, for pressing China to adjust its economic and trade measures, and to further extent, for helping narrow down the U.S. trade deficit.

What so far have been the consequences of this trade war for the U.S., China-U.S. trade, and even beyond anyway?

Even though the trade war was initiated by the U.S., with a declared purpose of managing China-U.S. unbalanced trade, a range of facts can tell that the relevant outcomes have gone to an opposite direction of the U.S. expectations. The U.S. domestic consumers since the trade war started, as generally agreed, have paid higher prices for some of their daily necessities. Apart from that, because of being disrupted by the trade war, China's total exports and imports with the U.S. in 2019 were down to 3.73 trillion RMB and by 10.7 percent. [3]

Nevertheless, even China-U.S. trade shrunk in

2019, China's imports and exports with the countries of the Association of Southeast Asian Nations (ASEAN) surged to 4.43 trillion RMB and by 14.1 percent, which made the ASEAN up to the second largest trading partners of China in 2019 by replacing the United States. Besides that, China's trade volumes with its major trading partners including the Europe Union and Japan as well as the countries along the Belt and Road route all raised by various percentage points.[4]

Overall, despite that China-U.S. trade decreased largely in 2019, China's total commodity trade in 2019 still increased to 31.54 trillion RMB, and by 3.4 percent, compared to its level of 2018.[5]

Therefore, we can say that China's total amount of trade in 2019 wasn't affected that much by the China-U.S. trade war. This outcome was contrary to some expectations and predictions in the U.S.. Meanwhile, the U.S. consumers, certain U.S. domestic companies, and other series of related sectors might have borne a lot of damages of this trade war.

Furthermore, the global industrial chains in some areas should have been affected as well by the trade wars and economic sanctions launched by the U.S. against other countries - though the author didn't notice any specific figures released concerning the assessment of the damages caused by the trade wars to the global industrial chains. It is worth notifying that around 90 percent of goods in international trade are transferred in the form of semi-products. This means that the industrial chains across the globe are closely interdependent, and most of the products in global trade are jointly made by a number of countries.[6] Therefore, the trade wars should have more or less created disruptions to the businesses of a number of transnational corporations.

Though the trade war has caused numerous discrepancies to China-U.S. economic and trade engagements over the past 2-3 years, the two countries, after having undergone more than 13 rounds of intensive negotiations, finally managed to reach a Phase One trade deal in January 2020, which was seen as an uneasy achievement of both countries.

The question now is that how likely the next U.S. administration would seek to proceed the Phase One trade deal? Also, what could be the possible policy direction of the next government on China-U.S. economic and trade issues?

In a recent interview with the New York Times, Biden revealed that his administration would temporarily keep the China-U.S. Phase One deal, and wouldn't seek to take any immediate actions including lifting the tariffs. He also added that his government would assess comprehensively of the Phase One deal, and in the meantime, consult with the U.S. traditional allies for the possibility of working out a joint strategy. Before then, he wouldn't make any personal judgment.[7]

From the information above, we could sense that the U.S. would attempt to pursue closer engagements with its allies on economic and trade issues to jointly deal with the common challenges in this area. Even though, it is not clear at the moment, how the U.S. would tend to move further its engagements with its allies, there could be a possibility that the U.S. may cooperate with its allies to form new rules as well as to jointly reform some of the old rules. For instance, the U.S. and the EU may tend to reform some of the rules within the WTO. However, given the differences between the U.S. and the EU on the matter of reforming the WTO as well as their disagreements on other series of issues in the economic and trade sphere, how they could manage to make a breakthrough on those matters is yet to be seen. Apart from that, for the U.S. economic engagements with its Asian allies, the U.S. might consider to join in the negotiations of the Comprehensive Progressive Trans-Pacific Partnerships (CPTPP), or it may tend to initiate new economic mechanisms.

Generally, the trend of the U.S. economic and trade policy wouldn't move away from multilateralism and multilateral institutions, because the U.S. would expect to rely on multilateral mechanisms to benefit the U.S. economy. Whatever rules, networks, and mechanisms will be newly formed or reformed, the goal is to make them better meet the U.S. needs.

Concerning China-U.S. bilateral economic ties, as usual, there could be many possibilities, which should also be closely linked with the U.S. engagements with its allies. We shouldn't exclude the likelihood that, in various occasions, the U.S. would attempt to align with other countries to manage China, given that the nature of the China-U.S. bilateral ties in certain areas will be driven by a combination of cooperation and competition. However, whether the U.S. allies will be able to accommodate the U.S. policies and moves, by taking into considerations their internal and external situations, should be another issue.

Another issue is that, from the U.S. perspective, the series of repercussions caused by the trade wars should have made the Biden team understand better that tough sanctions and measures cannot solve some of the fundamental problems faced by the U.S., as well as of the differences between the U.S. and other countries including China. No party can benefit from a constant confrontational relationship. Therefore, regardless of what economic and trade polices the next U.S. government would take, its biggest concern would be to solve problems rather than to create problems. By understanding this point well, there should be a bigger space for China and the U.S. to negotiate with regard to the implementation of their Phase One deal as well as other series of issues in the economic and trade sphere.

Technology

Alongside the China-U.S. disputes on economic and trade matters, the growing tension between the two countries in the area of technology has also drawn a lot of international attention. On 22 May and 26 August, the U.S. Department of Commerce subsequently announced to include 33 and 24 Chinese entities into the Entity List. Those entities being sanctioned mainly consist of Chinese technological companies, scientific research institutes, and universities. They usually have special expertise and knowledge in AI technology, cloud computing, communication, and aerospace science and technology etc. The U.S. side claimed that the entities being included in the Entity List have the potential to undermine the U.S. national security and foreign policy interests. Therefore, without the official permission of the U.S. Commerce Department, their ability to access to the U.S. technology, or to buy the products or components of certain products made with the U.S. technology, should be restricted.

In addition to the above, with regard to the specific cases of how the U.S. having dealt with the Chinese tech companies, the U.S. management of Huawei and TickTok has been two of the mostly concerned cases. Since 2018, a series of measures have been taken by the U.S. government to limit the regular business engagements between Huawei and the U.S. technological companies. The restrictive measures on Huawei have also affected a number of companies and entities which have cooperative relationships with Huawei from other parts of the world. Besides that, the U.S. government has subsequently set pressure on its allies and pushed them, through various ways, to restrain Huawei's cooperation with local companies on the 5G network construction. Despite the U.S. government ever, occasion by occasion, extended or softened certain restrictive measures concerning the Huawei case, the disputes are still going on, and the restrictions still impact on Huawei's business operations.

Regarding the U.S. government management of TickTok, a few months before the U.S. general election in early August, for national security concerns, the U.S. government announced a measure against TickTok - the Chinese technological company Bytedance, which is the parent company of TickTok, was pressed to make a deal with a U.S. company within 45 days by selling out part of TickTok's businesses, otherwise, the U.S. government would ban the operation of TickTok in the U.S.. Microsoft and Oracle were subsequently involved in negotiations with Bytedance. Later, Bytedance turned down Microsoft's offer, and made a decision to cooperate with Oracle on further negotiation of a deal. A deal so far hasn't been reached yet. After the U.S. government announcing the possible ban of TickTok, Bytedance has made a lot of efforts to defend the company's interests. So far the ban of TickTok's operation in the U.S. has postponed for a few times already.

Apart from the series of restrictions against the Chinese technological corporations, students' studying programme as well as scholarly exchanges and communications have been affected also.

By taking the above information into account, then how to understand about the U.S. actions against Chinese tech corporations and research institutes?

As generally agreed previously, the U.S. general election was part of the reasons behind certain tough measures taken by the U.S.. In addition to that, from the U.S. position, those series of policies and actions also reflected the urgency that the U.S. government sensed in terms of handling the number of issues it has been facing. This kind of mentality may be more accurately described as such - the more serious the problems are, the more urgent the U.S. government feels to deal with them, and the tougher the actions against others should be.

The failure of the government in bringing the coronavirus under control has made some of the challenges - such as the trust deficiency between the people and the government as well as the overall domestic economic situation - get worse.

Because of the mismanagement of internal and external challenges, the U.S. government has faced enormous pressure from the domestic political parties as well as from the U.S. public. Yet within a short period of time, it is not possible to find a better solution at the domestic level to manage all these issues suddenly emerged. Thus, the U.S. must have to seek solutions at the international level to offset the rising tension within the domestic society. From the U.S. government position, as far as it could manage to secure certain achievements at the international level such as making a trade deal or any other type of deals with other governments, or showing how strong and powerful in all respects the U.S. still is, the domestic pressure faced by the U.S. government should be eased a bit in certain degree. Under these circumstances, it is no surprising that China and the Chinese technological entities have become the main targets of the U.S. sanctions and measures.

Furthermore, from a broader and deeper perspective, the range of actions and measures taken by the U.S. over the past few years also indicated that the U.S. has been making efforts to adjust its overall strategies. With respect to the area of science and technology, China's investment and development in AI technology, online-communication, and aerospace technology etc. has made the U.S. feel threatened. The U.S. has long been in a leading position in science and technology from a general sense; and it has been proud of its great achievements in this spectrum. Therefore, it wouldn't allow other countries to surpass its capacity.

The U.S. general goal is to sustain its dominance in all major issue areas including economic and military capacity, education, research, communication, and science and technology. Therefore, the objective of launching trade wars and pressing other countries to adjust their economic policies and measures is to enhance and sustain the U.S. economic power; restricting scholarly exchanges and communications bears a purpose of keeping the U.S. dominance in education and research; taking actions against the Chinese technological firms and scientific research institutes aims to prevent China from surpassing the U.S. in technology and science; playing China's sovereign cards including the cards of Hong Kong,

Taiwan, Tibet, and Xinjiang carries a purpose of balancing the U.S. foreign and security policy interests. Thus, targeting the Chinese tech area just reflects part of the U.S. overall strategic adjustments.

However, some U.S. policy advisers seem to have ignored a fact that the things having made the U.S. strong are based on an open culture and environment. The Trump government aims to make the U.S. great. Nevertheless, it has attempted to achieve that purpose through applying a more confrontational, protectionist, and isolationist approach, as a result of that, the government has lost control on certain issues including the rising of more controversies and divisions at the domestic level as well as the worsening relationship with other countries in the international landscape.

Given the above background, what could be the next U.S. administration's approach in dealing with the U.S. cooperation and competition with China in the sphere of science and technology?

The priority for the next administration should be to bring issues back under control. It will adjust the U.S. policies and measures in engaging with other countries including its allies and its competitors. In the initial stage, a softer approach will likely be taken into account. That means, even though China-U.S. technological competition will not disappear, the next government will more likely apply a different approach, compared to that of the Trump government, to interact with China. How to avoid escalating the current situation will be a big concern for the next administration.

If the next U.S. government is able to achieve a relationship of coexistence with China, and in the meantime, to meet the interests of both countries along with their cooperation and competition in the field of science and technology, that should be a great achievement not only for China and the U.S. but also for the world, as such kind of practice made by China and the U.S could set a good example for other countries' cooperation and competition in this field as well.

To achieve this goal, an alternative solution would be to jointly work out certain regulations by the two large powers to properly manage their cooperation and disputes in the area of science and technology. Sound regulations can help guarantee fair competition and cooperation among tech corporations and institutions. If impartiality is absent, the disputes between China and the U.S. in the future cannot be easily handled.

Global Governance

China-U.S. possible cooperation and competition in various fields including the three areas just assessed above could affect the two countries' cooperation and coordination in global governance as well. The differences likely to remain between China and the U.S. in the sphere of global governance mainly consist of two aspects: the reform of some institutions and mechanisms, as well as the possible making of new rules, norms and mechanisms.

Over the past years, the shortcomings of some multilateral institutions have gradually appeared, as a result of that, certain international organizations haven't been able to better deal with the emerging challenges in the new century any longer. The functions of many institutions have become disputable - either they might face a challenge of being more effective or of being more legitimate; or they might have an enforcement problem. Though a lot of efforts have been made by some countries in promoting the reform of certain global institutions, partly due to the complexity of interests held by different powers within the relevant institutions, as well as to the shortcomings entrenched within the number of institutions themselves, so far not many good outcomes have been obtained in terms of pushing forward the reform process.

After the pandemic, major powers would see a further necessity to seek alternative solutions to press the reform of some international organizations and mechanisms in order to improve the global governance system as a whole, and more crucially, to make the system better serve their countries' needs. The future for a number of institutions might face a few possibilities: either some may find good solutions to complete at least part of their reforms; or they could be transformed in a way of being merged with or of being replaced by a series of new institutions and mechanisms, which are expected to have similar functions with the traditional ones yet likely with more effectiveness and functional capacity in enforcing decisions; or some institutions might face the pressure of being closed or of being not much relevant to the challenges in the new century.

How to make the series of multilateral international organizations stay more relevant to the fast changing world then? There are experts having proposed that, apart from continuing to apply some of the traditional means to push for reforms of the existing institutions and mechanisms, relevant countries and institutions are advised to find new alternative approaches to address the problems existed within the number of traditional institutions. As Ian Goldin ever argued more broadly, "we need to look for more imaginative solutions - beyond the usual suspects - and leverage the enormous potential that comes through globalization and today's hyperconnectivity."[8]

In order to improve the global governance system, and make the system meet the interests of as more states and also various stakeholders in the system as possible, greater and more transparent participation from a wide range of sectors within the societies is very necessary. The following part would focus on the exploration of the role of states, of international institutions, and of other variety of sectors in terms of their possible contributions to regional and global problem-solving.

For the number of international organizations to remain more relevant to addressing today's challenges, they may have to make some fundamental changes beyond their usual way of thinking or of handling the matters they used to face.

Many multilateral organizations were established a few decades ago. Given the increasing diversity and frequency of emerging challenges in today's world, the set of institutions may have to check out whether their organizational objectives or mandates have been outdated, and then whether there is a need to adjust part of them. Besides that, the knowledge and expertise base within the international organizations usually follows certain fixed benchmarks, standards or principles. In order to bring fresh ideas and more creative solutions into the organizations, the series of international institutions may take into account the act of breaking their usual standards for selecting. For instance, they can increase the share of knowledge expertise from developing countries or invite the expertise and practitioners from other variety of professional circles to jointly deal with some of the most challenging issues entrenched within certain multilateral international institutions. Furthermore, some institutions may need to consider whether their enforcement mechanisms need to be amended in order to increase their enforcement capacities. They may put a question like this: for any defiance of a binding agreement by a particular member of the relevant institutions, whether the institutions have any alternative rescuing measures and solutions to handle this issue. [9] Anyway, these are just part of the issues that some international institutions need to take into consideration in relation to pushing forward the reform process.

From the perspective of a large circle of non-state and non-institutional sectors including the business sector, civil society groups, transnational and trans-governmental networks, research centres and networks, and the private sector etc., they can be in a position of helping facilitate platforms for generating public debates, through which, to press states to abide by their commitments or to influence policy-making.

Apart from that, they could also play a role of coordination among states, or between states and other various organizational sectors in a way to help mitigate the discrepancies of interests among diverse range of stakeholders.

From the position of states, effective cooperation and coordination among states, in particular, the major powers should still be the key in promoting problem-solving in international dimensions. Very often, states are the most crucial contributors to make the international system work better. Yet due to certain conflicts of interests, states could also become the key blockers in terms of undermining international cooperation, and of affecting the implementation of global institutional decisions. Under such circumstances, the effectiveness and enforcement capacity of certain international organizations could be compromised.

In the new globalized age, in order to minimize the repercussions caused by states' rejection to their international commitments, or to reduce the possibility of states' defiance of international decisions and resolutions, the principle of "A Coalition of the Willing"[10] rather than that of intimidating and pressing by big powers to smaller powers, could be taken as an alternative solution to help forge a new means of coordination and cooperation in the process of pushing forward reforms of certain institutions. For instance, states, in keeping up with the changes and their needs, could seek new possible options such as forging new mechanisms together with other nations having similar interests in whatever particular issue areas. In this case, the issue of whether the new initiatives are formal or informal shouldn't be the main concern, rather, efficiency and flexibility should be more important.

"A Coalition of the Willing" can also be applied in helping address some of the shortcomings remained in certain multilateral organizations, or in helping promote changes in relation to some main global challenges such as the issue of climate change. As far as states are willing to make their commitments to promoting reforms and changes, they should be ready to give up part of their interests. Reaching a consensus, under such circumstances, should be relatively easier. As Goldin put, "For issues of global gravity, the coalition of the willing may be persuaded that the domestic cost of inaction is greater than the potential benefits of a more comprehensive international distribution of the burdens of action."[11]

Moreover, promoting regionalism should also be an alternative solution for states to better manage global problems. Regionalism and regional organizations could serve as good complements to multilateralism and international institutions. "Regional economic arrangement may boost multilateral openness through incentives for expansion and improving efficiency through simply reducing the number of members involved in negotiations. For some other issues, such as agricultural trade reform, going from a regional-based agreement to a global one may well prove an effective stepping stone." [12]

Furthermore, great powers' coordination and cooperation should be emphasized in promoting global problem-solving and making the global governance system work better. Regardless of what the objectives are - either for moving forward reforms of traditional multilateral institutions, or for forging new multilateral rules and regulations, or for managing other series of emerging challenges in the regional and global dimensions, the key is for great powers including China and the U.S. to work together by applying a set of new coordination and cooperation measures and principles, rather than fall apart on managing these core areas of challenges.

Conclusion

This study has assessed the prospects of cooperation and competition between China and the U.S. in four main areas: foreign and security policy, economic and trade issues, technology, and global governance. Though other areas of issues such as climate change, pandemic, cyber-security, counter-terrorism, and the rule of law etc., with respect to the overall China-U.S. bilateral ties, are also of equally significance, generally the four major areas having just examined by this study should have been able to reflect a general trend of the China-U.S. bilateral ties in the coming years, which is that the China-U.S. bilateral relationship will be mixed by collaboration and competition. The nature of a relationship with cooperation and competition means that there will be a bigger space and a higher probability for even closer engagements between the two countries. Meanwhile, certain degree of differences and disputes might be raised accordingly as well; and on some issues, there might be more intensive bargaining and negotiating involved.

Over the past more than 7 decades since the end of the second World War, China and the U.S. have managed to surpass a huge amount of difficulties in all core issue areas, concerning their bilateral relationship, from complete isolation to closer interdependence. Every time when the two countries managed to jointly overcome some disputes and differences, China-U.S. bilateral collaboration was upgraded to a new level. In fact, the joint efforts of China and the U.S. in solving their bilateral challenges have benefited not only the two big powers but also the whole globe.

Currently, by standing at a new historical starting point and in the face of a great deal of new national, regional, and global challenges, there is a need for the two major powers to make continuous efforts to better manage their collaboration and competition, and ultimately to make China-U.S. bilateral ties reach a status of coexistence. By doing so, their bilateral engagements would contribute to the shaping of a new world order, as many have anticipated, on the one hand; and their interactions should be able to enrich both the theories and practices of a new type of great power relations as well as of a new type of international relations on the other hand.

Notes

1. Interview to the U.S. former Secretary of State Dr. Henry Kissinger by the Bloomberg Editor-in-Chief John Micklethwait on 16 November 2020 upon an online convening of the New Economy Forum 2020. *The Paper.* 21 November 2020.
http://www.thepaper.cn/newsDetail_forward_100892 44

2. China-U.S. trade data for the year of 2018 was released by the Ministry of Commerce of the People's Republic of China during its Regular Press Conference on 17 January 2019. *Guancha.* 17 January 2019.

http://www.guancha.cn/economy/2019_01_17_48727
6.shtml

3. Trade data for the year of 2019 was released by the General Administration of Customs of the People's Republic of China. *Sohu.* 14 January 2020. http://www.sohu.com/a/366906629_557006

4. Ibid.

5. Ibid.

6. Data was cited from Yao Yang (2020). "How to Understand the Dual Circulation of the Chinese Economy". *Sina.* 13 October 2020. finance.sina.com.cn/zl/china/2020-10-13/zl-iiznezxr5790402.shtml

7. Interview to the U.S. President-elect Joe Biden by the New York Times. *Tecent.* 3 December 2020. http://finance.qq.com/a/20201203/000358.htm

8. Ian Goldin (2013). *Divided Nations-Why Global Governance Is Failing, and What We Can Do about It.* Oxford University Press. pp106.

9. Ian Goldin has more discussions on advising the measures and solutions for promoting reforms of certain multilateral international institutions including adjusting the mandates and knowledge base of the institutions. For more details on the relevant measures, please see chapter three of Ian Goldin's book *Divided Nations-Why Global Governance Is Failing, and What We Can Do about It.*

10. The phrase of "Coalition of the Willing" was borrowed from Ian Goldin. See Ian Goldin *Divided Nations-Why Global Governance Is Failing, and What We Can Do about It. PP.107*

11. Ibid. PP.108

12. Ibid. PP.91

Chapter 3

China and the United States on the Coronavirus and Beyond

I. The Coronavirus, Non-traditional Security, and Ideology

"Coronavirus" has been a worldwide key word over the past around one month plus two weeks. Reporting and discussions related to it have been occupying a much larger space compared with that of other areas of issues in the media outlets. Till 8 March, the total number of confirmed cases of the coronavirus across the globe has surpassed 106893, over 3000 people have died, more than 100 countries have been influenced, and South Korea, Italy, Iran, Japan, France and Germany so far have been the countries outside China being most severely affected.

At the very beginning of the outbreak, many might have thought that it was probably mainly an issue of China - an imminent threat that China must have to face and deal with very quickly and effectively. Nonetheless, with the fast spread of the disease as well as with the difficulty in controlling it, it quickly turned into an issue of the globe, and almost the whole world must need to pay special attentions to it.

There have been some worries, anxieties, and pressure going on along with the developing of the coronavirus. People are uncertain about how the situation will be evolving especially outside China in the coming weeks and maybe even months. Some debates and discussions in relation to the coronavirus, and also to other series of issues beyond the virus have been raised in the meantime. This piece would pick up a few core debatable points to briefly analyse. They mainly consist of China's role in combating the coronavirus, the issue of non-traditional security, and the matter of ideology.

China's Role in Combating the Coronavirus

At the very early stage of the outbreak, most countries had appeared to be in an observing mood toward the virus by looking at carefully of how China would handle this. Within a few days, with the quick changing of the situation, many countries started to take certain light actions including deploying aircraft to take back their own citizens from the outbreak centre Wuhan.

Alongside the evolving situation of the pandemic, different voices have been raised up regarding china's role in responding to the virus - positive or negative. On the one hand, China has received a wide range of support from a number of countries, organizations, charities, private sectors, and other series of national and transnational agencies. For instance, the officials of the World Health Organization (WHO) spoke highly of China's contribution to the world in combating the coronavirus. On the other hand, there were certain media and people having shown negative attitude toward China's handling of the case. Some accused China of violating human rights when the Wuhan city was locked down, criticized the tough measures taken by China in dealing with the virus, and at a later stage started to name the coronavirus as a "Chinese Virus". Some may even have thought about taking advantage of the challenging situation faced by China.

With the pandemic situation getting worse at the global level, some accusations and critics became futile, as the uncontrollable situation made some realize that China made the right decision to apply quick and effective measures to curb the spread of the virus.

China has made enormous efforts and sacrifices in combating the virus domestically, and also has greatly contributed to the global efforts in fighting the pandemic. Along with the anti-pandemic process, despite different voices having come up, China's efforts and contribution have been well recognized by the international community.

China's contribution lies in the fact that China, as the initial centre of the outbreak, accumulated valuable experiences in curbing the disease, which can be served as references for other countries to manage the similar situations in line with the real conditions of their countries.

Fighting the virus can be a test to a country's leadership, system, and governance capacity. Leadership, fast reaction, well-planning, and organization from the top down to the bottom and among all range of sectors, as well as the effective communication among all these sectors can be of great significance to win the battle. Generally, the Chinese leadership, various levels of government departments, security sector, hospitals, communities, volunteers, and all other institutions and sectors involved in this battle have done remarkable jobs and made tremendous achievements in bringing the epidemic under control in a short period of time.

More precisely, China, in responding to the virus, has acted very quickly - it timely worked out strict and effective measures to control the spread of the virus including limiting people's outdoor activities, travel, and transportation etc.; in only ten days two hospitals were established in Wuhan; and with the growing number of patients, it quickly deployed other type of buildings and blocks in Wuhan to set up necessities and facilities inside these buildings and blocks as temporary camps for collecting patients with light symptoms. Along with the process of fighting the disease, government officials as well as others who were dereliction of their duties or failed to react properly in the process of combating the disease were removed from their positions.

While ensuring certain measures is still in place in accordance with the evolving situation of the coronavirus in different regions of China and of the globe, China has been gradually promoting its economic and business activities back to normal. Generally, China has responded timely, effectively, and properly to the outbreak of the coronavirus.

In addition, the great efforts made by China at the very early stage of the outbreak had actually prevented the virus from rising to a much larger scale both within China and on the global level. China's efforts were supposed to have bought valuable time for other countries to prepare well in handling the coronavirus issue. Unfortunately, a great number of countries hadn't paid enough attention to the seriousness of the virus by then. As a consequence, they failed to catch the best time made for them to stop the large scale spread of the disease later.

The Issue of Non-traditional Security

States would usually pay more attention to issues related to traditional security while downplaying the threats in the non-traditional security area. They generally think that increasing military spending, building alliance relationships, and applying balance of power tactics would make them safer. However, history has proved that these measures and tactics wouldn't make states more secure. In ancient times, the Greek city-states had already started to develop alliance systems and deploy containment strategies in order to maintain the balance of power among the Greek city-states, nonetheless, those hadn't stopped Sparta and Athens from going to war. Over the past number of centuries, by applying similar tactics, states have failed to prevent numerous wars and conflicts.

Non-traditional security issues like infectious disease, climate change, and ecological imbalance wouldn't get as more attention as traditional security does, mostly because threats generated by these areas of issues usually need a process to develop and they don't seem to be imminent. Thus, the damages and severity resulted by non-traditional security threats are very often being ignored or postponed. Also there generally appears to be a lack of enough and effective cooperation on both regional and global levels to jointly address the potential challenges in the non-traditional security area.

The world has borne some consequences already led by non-traditional security challenges over the past recent years. For instance, with regard to the repercussions of the infectious disease, the world had dealt with the outbreak of SARS in 2003, and of EBOLA in 2014. Now the world has to face the threat of COVID-19.

The outbreak of the coronavirus once again sent out a warning to global leaders, policy makers, practitioners, researchers, and advocacy groups that states and a wide variety of partners and groups need to come together to deepen collaboration in research concerning the potential challenges in the non-traditional security field, as well as to enhance cooperation in developing better technologies, mechanisms, norms and rules to limit the similar incidents to happen in the future.

Another lesson learnt from this epidemic could be that there is a need for both the ordinary people and governments to re-consider issues related to development and the quality of life - seeking quality, inclusive and more balanced development, limiting the exploitation and consumption of resources, respecting the environment we humans live, and respecting all the species living in this world would make humans' life better, more secure, and more sustainable. In addition, high standards of living and quality life, from the material sense, are neither about achieving things without limits, nor are about meeting human demands without constraints.

Upon the outbreak of this coronavirus, the Chinese authority has tightened relevant regulations to ban the trading and consuming of certain wild animals. Scientists are still studying whether the virus originally came from the wild animals or not. The final research finding out of this might be significant. The more significant issue is that there is a necessity for the ordinary people and various levels of governments in both China and other countries to take very seriously of the protection and consumption of wild animals. This kind of seriousness is mostly concerned with the enforcement of law once certain rules and regulations are in place.

On Ideological Difference

Along with the Coronavirus, the issue of ideology has once again been raised. Some questioned whether the socialist system or the capitalist democratic system is more effective in dealing with the emergencies like this epidemic.

Ideological difference was ever taken as a big issue in a certain period of the past century when the two big camps - the socialist system and the capitalist camp - competed for supremacy and dominance at the global stage. With the disintegration of the former Soviet Union, as well as with the shaping of a more globalized world, the influence of ideological difference has been gradually lessened in international relations. Nevertheless, sometimes it could still be an issue for some nowadays, who might take this as an excuse to criticize the political and economic system of a socialist country.

This piece in response would once again raise the point that the socialist system developed by China today is not the one adopted by the then China, the former Soviet Union, and other former socialist countries. The socialist system adopted in the past by those socialist countries was generally lack of flexibility and efficiency, without having timely adjusted their countries' policies and measures to make them more adaptable to the market demands as well as to the changing domestic and international situations.

China learnt from its past mistakes, and then has started to adopt a policy of reform and opening up since the late 1970s. By taking into account the different characteristics and requirements of its national development stages, as well as in line with the changing international situation, China has gradually developed a market-oriented economy, and in the meantime, has made its political system be more supportive to the economic activities.

For those who still see the ideology as a big matter in today's world, while respecting their views, this analysis meanwhile would assume that they don't seem to have seen the changes and improvements of some socialist countries with a fair, dialectical, and historical lens. It appears that the kind of socialism criticized by some today is still the one that ever existed in the past century.

By the way, the points expressed here do not tend to be in favour of or in contrary to a particular political or economic system. It would rather support a view - which has already been supported by many - All countries, big or small, should have their rights and freedoms to choose their political and economic systems and development paths, which are most suitable to their countries' conditions.

Under the current circumstances, ideological difference shouldn't be taken as a big matter to prevent countries, socialist nations or democratic states, from taking the most effective measures to fight the virus. When human life and health being threatened in this particular period of time, there is a need for democracies to temporarily downplay their concerns on certain dogmatic values and to take the most proper measures to deal with the virus.

II. Practical Measures in Fighting the COVID-19 Pandemic

The world is right now undergoing a serious health crisis caused by the COVID-19 pandemic. As some leaders have claimed, "We are in a war".

Till 29 March, the confirmed cases of the coronavirus globally in total have reached to more than 600,000, and over 30,000 people have been reported dead. The centre of the epidemic around this time has shifted from China to Europe, and then to the United States. Over the past few days, the number of confirmed infections across the European continent and within the United States has been seen a dramatic surge. The U.S. now has claimed more than 123,750 cumulative infections. The confirmed cases in Italy, Spain, Germany, France, and the United Kingdom have respectively surpassed 92,472, 73,235, 57,695, 37,575, and 17,089. Iran is the country being mostly affected by the pandemic in the Middle-East with over 35,408 people having contracted the disease.

People would generally agree that it is a bit too late for some countries to take actions now, and that they have missed the best time bought by China in the very early stage of the outbreak. It can be recalled that when the Wuhan city was shut down on 23 January, China only had 830 confirmed cases, and by then China already started to take prompt actions to curb the spread of the disease. Yet because of the severity of the virus alongside people's higher requirements in cross-city traveling upon the Chinese Lunar New Year period, the increasingly tougher measures didn't stop the number of infections rising very quickly, till the end of February with the number of confirmed cases almost approaching to 80,000; but after then the number of daily infections has been seen a steady drop. Till 29 March, the number of cumulative infections in the mainland China has totalled 81,470, with 75,770 recoveries, 3,304 fatalities, and less than 3,500 remaining in the hospital.

For countries with high numbers of confirmed cases right now like some European countries and the U.S., apart from being committed to adhering to more concrete measures, there don't seem to be any better solutions out there at the moment, and presumably they may need much longer time to finally get over this.

Anyway, the current difficult situation didn't stop the national governments and international organizations making attempt to address the series of challenges led by the COVID-19 pandemic. An extraordinary G20

Leaders' Summit was convened via a video link on 26 March. A series of international organizations including the WTO, IMF, WB, and the UN etc. this time were also invited to participate in the meeting. The summit centred on calling on the G20 countries and international organizations to work together with confidence and unity to defeat the coronavirus pandemic, as well as to take all necessary means to minimize the social, economic, and financial impacts of the pandemic, safeguard the global economy, restore market confidence, protect the global demand and supply chains, and ensure financial stability through coordinated global efforts.

Out of the leaders' summit, the G20 countries and the participating international organizations reached a common understanding on jointly addressing the pandemic by offering policy advice and funding support. The financial ministers, central bank governors and the representatives of the relevant international organizations will make coordinated efforts to deliver the relevant tasks. From the financial aspect, they agreed to inject 5 trillion USD into the global economy to help countries combat the coronavirus pandemic. Developing and the least developed countries with weaker public health response systems, the vulnerable groups, and the micro-, small, and medium-sized enterprises will be gravely concerned by the joint global efforts in this special period of time.

In addition to the joint international efforts made by the G20 countries and international organizations in addressing the repercussions of the coronavirus, on the national level, the governments in various countries and regions are believed to have subsequently issued policy measures including economic stimulus packages to help fight the epidemic. For instance, the U.S. government decided to release 2 trillion USD to combat the disease.

Overall, there have been policies, measures, and support out there on both international and national levels to help address the coronavirus. Meanwhile, this article would in addition emphasize a point that without enough support of the people in relevant countries, these social, economic, and financial measures are not likely to achieve their efficiencies as early as they are expected. Therefore, one of the core issues for winning the battle against the pandemic ultimately very much relies on the support and cooperation of the people. The experiences accumulated by some countries including South Korea, China and Singapore etc. in bringing the worsening situation under control in a relatively short period of time have already proved this point. It is a people's war against the pandemic.

Apart from the list of practical experiences shared already by the public institutes of various governments as well as by other wide range of sectors, here this piece would once again highlight, in a very simple way, a few pieces of useful practices accumulated by China to hopefully serve as references for other countries in their fighting against the disease.

First, it is in need to set up an organizational framework consisting of a leading group and relevant personnel. This is supposed to lead and supervise the overall anti-epidemic work, and to ensure the smooth communication, coordination, and arrangement in relation to all aspects of responsibilities and tasks against the pandemic from the top down to the bottom in general terms. It is assumed that the governments of some foreign countries should have already done detailed arrangements on this part of the work. One of the very crucial matters in the whole process concerning the efforts made by them is to ensure information transparency, which is conducive to improving the efficiency of all aspects of work.

Second, abiding by the principle of "early finding out, early reporting / testing, early isolating / quarantining, and early rescuing / treatment" in terms of dealing with the people with symptoms. More precisely, this principle means that, as earliest as possible, finding out all those with symptoms, diagnosing and testing them, tracking and quarantining all those having been exposed to the confirmed cases, and rescuing the infected patients timely.

Third, there is a necessity to unite the people and gain their support and cooperation. In facing the pandemic, certain foreign governments might have found a bit difficult to carry this part of the work. One of the examples is that the public officers encountered the difficulties sometimes in persuading people to stay home or in stopping them from participating in group activities. We have seen from the media that the government officials and police officers in certain European countries have already devoted a great deal of efforts in performing this duty.

In China's practices, majority of the work in relation to minding people about their social distancing and human to human contacts etc., has been done by the community workers or volunteers. The police officers during this special time have mainly been deployed to handle the kind of people who broke the law or refused to obey certain anti-pandemic regulations and measures temporarily issued by the governments.

It is assumed that the communities, universities, councils, and other various places in foreign countries should have their service centres as well. Local governments or city councils, if necessary, are suggested to work closely with the service centres to temporarily recruit a large number of volunteers living inside the relevant communities or nearby to join the governments' effort in fighting the disease at the community levels. The main tasks of the community workers and volunteers are involved in better meeting the needs of the local citizens including persuading them to adhere to certain rules, as well as helping them get or deliver the daily living necessities and so on.

Fourth, wearing a face mask should be a must. All people especially those currently living in the most severely infected regions by the pandemic are strongly advised to wear face masks in public places.

A great number of people have already been vaccinated. It is assumed that in the first half of the year 2021, the vaccines will be ready for public injection at a much larger scale on the global level. Certain countries like China have been busy with doing the relevant arrangements on this. The availability of the vaccines means that the world has seen a hope there toward finally defeating the COVID-19 pandemic.

III. The Coronavirus, the United States, and the World

By 4 May, the number of confirmed cases of the COVID-19 in the United States has totalled more than 1,157,687, and over 67,674 people have died so far. Since the outbreak began, the U.S. government has subsequently issued a series of measures and policies to combat the pandemic including establishing a COVID-19 Special Action Group, banning foreign citizens' traveling to the U.S., tightening border control and quarantine measures, suspending legal immigration to the U.S. for 60 days, cutting interest rate, and releasing big stimulus packages to help the economy etc. Nevertheless, certain measures and policies haven't prevented the situation from getting worse gradually. The number of confirmed cases and of fatalities has kept growing, and the turning point of it still hasn't reached yet. So, what are the reasons behind the deteriorating situation related to the coronavirus in the U.S. today? People have been debating on this. Some argued that the ignorance of the U.S. government, in the early stage of the outbreak, to the seriousness of the disease, plus the improper handling of the health crisis in the later steps, have mainly contributed to the worsening situation today. *The Washington Post* released a long piece at the end of March to have listed how the U.S. administration has step by step failed to perform its duties to contain the virus. Meanwhile, there have been some officials in the U.S. making attempts to shift the blames in relation to the COVID-19 on to China. They think that China should take the blame for having transmitted the virus to the U.S. One of the U.S. state governors even sued China over this, and demanded China to compensate for the U.S. losses. A memo very recently uncovered by the U.S. press showed that the U.S. government ever worked out a specific strategy on how to play the blame games. Around the same time, there have been other series of discussions on what has led to the worsening situation of the coronavirus in the United States. This piece will try to analyse the issue of what might have been behind the deteriorating pandemic situation in the U.S. from a theoretical, ideological, and systemic perspective, and further to explore more broadly of whether and in what way the pandemic could have an impact on the world order as well as on the globalization process.

Cause behind the Worsening Pandemic Situation in the U.S.

While agreeing with some practical views made by many observers, this analysis would from a theoretical perspective add a point that the overwhelming influence of the liberal ideology within the U.S. society might have played a part in contributing to the worsening pandemic situation in the U.S. today. Being liberal is good. Actually, the author of this analytical piece values highly of the meritorious propositions of liberalism including its advocating for free and creative thinking, its propensity to peace rather than to conflict, and its emphasis on the significance of international law, norms, international institutions, and other variety of non-state actors in the prospect of contributing to problem-solving as well as to regional and global peace and prosperity. However, being liberal without proper limits would risk leading to sever consequences such as deregulation.

Regarding the connection between the liberal ideology and the U.S. approach in handling the coronavirus, the influence of the liberal ideology to the U.S. society can be observed from both the government and individual dimensions. From the government level, in the process of the U.S. dealing with the virus, a lot of voices have been coming up in the meantime - the voices could be from the health experts, medical staff, the officials of the Centre for

Disease Control and Prevention (CDC), the president, the secretaries, the economic advisers to the president, and the state governors and so on. Nevertheless, some of the voices, instead of paying more attention to people's lives and health, confused with each other, and probably even carried other special purposes. For instance, the CDC official, at the end of February, claimed that the risks of the coronavirus transmission were obvious, while the economic adviser to the president, at the same time, pointed out that the virus had already been contained.

Though there have been a lot of talking going on publicly on the government level, it doesn't seem to be clear who is in charge of the real matter. The general impression to the outside world is that there has been a lack of effective communication and coordination among those who take in charge of the range of issues in relation to the virus. For example, even for a very simple matter - whether the Americans should wear face masks in public or not, or whether there is a need to import face masks from a foreign country, relevant officials may need to take two or three weeks and maybe even longer time to discuss and decide on it. Therefore, even though some sectors such as the CDC, the hospitals, and a wide variety of others may have started to take actions in the very early stage of the outbreak, ultimately, their early efforts haven't made much difference in terms of helping alter the overall pandemic situation in the U.S. After all, the lack of sound coordination and proper control has undermined the effective implementation of the relevant measures and policies, and ultimately contributed to the deteriorating situation in the U.S.. In a very short period of time, the centre of the COVID-19 had shifted from Europe to the U.S., and within only around five weeks from the final week of March to the end of April, the total number of confirmed cases of the COVID-19 in the U.S. had quickly surged from about 120, 000 to more than 1,000,000.

From the individual dimension, as having been influenced by the liberal ideology, a great number of people seemingly have lost their crisis consciousness. They don't seem to be worried that much about the spread of the disease. Even though the government issued the quarantine measure and warned about the severity of the pandemic, a large proportion of Americans still chose to ignore the series of warnings. The growing number of infections and of fatalities didn't stop the group-gathering activities beside the beach. More recently, because of the U.S. economy having been severely hit by the coronavirus, many Americans lost their jobs, a large group of people then marched on to the street to protest against the quarantine measure and demand for freedom.

Overall, the delay in issuing the quarantine measure, the government's inability in fully implementing it, plus the public non-cooperation to it have seriously compromised the efforts made by a variety of sectors in the process of combating the pandemic.

In addition to the above factor, the distrust given by the U.S. public to both the government and certain media has also played a role in leading to the worsening situation today. Then what caused the deficiency of trust by the people to the government? This assumingly should have a relevance to the U.S. political culture. The purpose of the political structures and organizations is supposed to better serve the people. However nowadays the U.S. politics appears to have become a strategic platform for the U.S. elite, politicians, and interest groups to compete for supremacy in order to gain their best interests. For the media, even though they claimed themselves to be free media and press, still a great number of them may have actually been supported by large interest groups. They could be used by some special interest groups as tools against other groups. In that case, how could it be possible for some of the media to be free and fair? Under such circumstances, it is not surprising that a great number of Americans nowadays have lost their trust in both the government and certain media. This kind of deficiency of trust among the public could also partly explain why a lot of Americans have chosen to dismiss the government's warning about the danger of the COVID-19. Obviously, without enough support of the people, the efforts made by all devoted sectors in fighting the pandemic would be undermined.

Overall, the COVID- 19 could have raised a number of issues for policy-makers, business people, and the representatives from a wide variety of sectors to think about more deeply. The most pressing one should be related to the short-term and long-term impacts of the coronavirus on various countries as well as on the global structure. The U.S. strategist Dr. Henry Kissinger on 3 April argued in an article published by *The Wall Street Journal* that "When the Covid-19 pandemic is over, many countries' institutions will be perceived as having failed. Whether this judgment is objectively fair is irrelevant. The reality is the world will never be the same after the coronavirus. To argue now about the past only makes it harder to do what has to be done."[1] Then we might see a different world in the post-COVID-19 pandemic era. Is that really going to happen? If so, how would the new global structure be like in the future? What global governance system would be more suitable to pave the way for the re-shaping of a new global structure? And what would be the trend of globalization? The next section will try to answer these questions.

Coronavirus and the World Order

Some observers have already shared their views on the issues raised above recently through the media coverage. One of the views is that the world will likely turn from a unipolar into a bipolar order, and the U.S. and China will be the two major poles. The relationship between this two will not be like the one between the U.S. and the former Soviet Union during the Cold War era, though a number of other countries might still take side between the great powers in different occasions.

This analytical piece would alternatively add a point that, given the potentiality of the emerging economies, the undeniable capability of some developed countries as well as the increasing role of non-state actors, the world might be far more complicated than just being bipolar or unipolar. Also, it is not certain whether the world will go to a bipolar or multipolar structure in the near future. This kind of complexity partly can be illustrated by the continuous growing role of non-state actors, and the non-state actors will likely join states' efforts in contributing to the forging of a new global framework.

In addition to that, in the area of global governance, regionalism might become more important in both theoretical and substantial terms in the future. That means regional development across the globe might become a very crucial force in driving changes on both regional and global levels. In that case, countries in various regions may have less interest in choosing side between global powers from either the economic or the security perspective. They might be more concerned about linking their real interests with regional powers.

Apart from the above, other series of questions in relation to the global structure have also been going on, one of which is that whether developing countries and emerging economies such as China after the pandemic could replace the role of developed countries like the U.S. in the process of shaping a new world order as well as of driving globalization?

This piece generally shares a number of analysts' views on this issue that it will be very unlikely for developing countries like China to replace the role of developed countries like the United States in the near term. Even if China's GDP surpasses that of the U.S., yet in many areas such as education, think tanks, science, and technology etc., China will still likely lag behind of the U.S.. Therefore, the role of the U.S. cannot be replaced in the near future. Most importantly, this article would maintain a view that, even if China becomes the most powerful country, it will not have an intention to replace the U.S. position, China's non-intention of doing that is more of an issue related to the Chinese culture and philosophy, which are far beyond the realist way of thinking about international relations.

The current system, in particular, the global economic system was forged under the U.S. leadership after WWII, and designed to better serve the interest of an U.S.-led world. Nevertheless, over the past decades, with the changing regional and international environment, the efficiency and fairness of a number of institutions and mechanisms under the current framework have been questioned. To better deal with the new issues emerged in today's world, the current system needs to be restructured. Many institutions and mechanisms are in need to get into a reform process. The task of restructuring the global system cannot be done by developed countries alone. It needs the joint efforts of both developed and developing nations in order to overcome the shortcomings existed in the old system, and further develop a fairer and more balanced system.

Coronavirus and the Globalization Trend

For the prospect of globalization process, the overall trend presumably in the future is for countries to seek a right balance between regulation and deregulation. There could be a possibility that protectionism in some countries will continue to raise its head and last for some time before these countries are ready to open themselves further to face the uncertainties of globalization. In that case, international free trade driven by the liberal ideology might once again be challenged, just like what had happened in late 1960s and early 1970s, by then the free movement of capital across borders had threatened the Bretton Woods fixed exchange rate regime, and finally led to the collapse of the regime. In response to that crisis, the U.S. then policy-makers, after having experienced the difficulties driven by a protectionist policy in the initial stage, made a decision to encourage private sectors to join international cooperation and play more important roles in cross-border economic and financial activities. Meanwhile, a series of attempts made by the U.S. in dealing with that crisis had also paved the way for the forging of a neo-liberal school of thought.

Now in facing the COVID-19 pandemic, given the difference of nature between an infectious disease and a number of crises happened in the past, the previous crisis management measures led by a liberal ideology cannot work out well obviously.

Besides that, another issue worth noticing is that the content of globalization has been changing over the past decades. Globalization process at the current stage is different from the one the world had experienced in the past century, because the issue areas the world has to face and the type of participating actors in the globalization process have been widened. Transnational corporations and international organizations had played a major role in driving the globalization process in its early stage, while nowadays in addition to transnational corporations, a great circle of other actors even including individuals have participated in the globalization process. Under such circumstances, the globalization trend cannot be prevented, and protectionism cannot go that far. If so, then how possibly would the liberal school of thought affect the globalization process as well as policy-making in the coming years?

One of the prospects could be that the world will see a bit more constrained liberalism, which basically means that some governments may tend to gain a bit more control of their business and economic activities in particular their overseas business operations. In fact, this trend has already started to take place since a few years back. Currently, upon the spread of the coronavirus as well as its great impact on the U.S. economy, a number of U.S. officials have felt the urgency to direct the U.S. big companies to move their operations out of China. The U.S. government has even offered to compensate the U.S. companies for whatever costs they might have.

By taking into account a number of factors including the market size of China, the labour force efficiency, as well as the consideration of profitability, though it is not certain whether the numerous attempts made by the U.S. government in persuading some of its businesses to move out of china will be able to succeed or not, at least we have seen this trend that some governments would aim to get their businesses a bit more under control in order to deal with the uncertainties in this more globalized world.

On this issue, a generally common view shared by a number of commentators is that completely leaving out of China will be very unlikely. The probable case could be that certain industries may consider diversifying their business operations by relocating part of them to other markets in order to secure some certainties.

In the meantime, to better cope with the possible upcoming uncertainties of globalization, this analysis would finally share the following points.

There is no fixed and single solution to the variety of global problems, as the world is full of complexities, uncertainties, and confusions; and these matters keep changing and interacting with each other. The only certainty is that the world is always driven by a mixture of theories and practices, and of material and non-material factors. Policy-making is based on politicians' understanding to certain thoughts and ideologies, as well as to the various phenomena and practices happening in the real world. Very often, only one school of thought may not be enough to help understand well the complexities the world faces. Interpreting the series of phenomena may need a hybrid approach consisting of a few schools of thoughts at the same time. Apart from that, one special idea or thought might be worked out well under certain conditions and in a particular period of time. Yet when the time changes; and the conditions are altered, the same theory might not be fully applicable any more. Under these circumstances, in order to better understand the changing situation and further solve the number of problems to possibly happen in the future, politicians, experts, practitioners, and a wider circle of other actors, who are mostly concerned about certain areas of global issues, might need to adjust their positions accordingly and shift their way of thinking from one to another.

After all, for all type of actors, states or non-states, an advisable solution to cope with the uncertainties of globalization in the post-pandemic era should be to seek an appropriate balance based on their understanding to the important factors around, and to try not to go extreme.

Notes

1.See Kissinger Henry (2020). "The Coronavirus Pandemic Will Forever Alter the World Order". Remarks by Dr. Henry Kissinger originally released by *The Wall Street Journal* on 3 April 2020. *Xinjingbao.* https://baijiahao.baidu.com/s?id=1663314191540020 269&wfr=spider&for=pc

Chapter 4

China and the United States on Taiwan and Hong Kong

I. On the Taiwan Local Election

On 11 Jan 2020, the Taiwan local election concluded with the re-election of the current leader. Right after this result came out, the Chinese authority re-affirmed China's position on the Taiwan issue by stating that "regardless of what happens in Taiwan, the basic fact won't change - there is only one China in the world and Taiwan is part of China."

Meanwhile, among a wide range of circles including the academic field and the media, there have been a lot of discussions on this issue mostly focusing on the causes of Cai's re-election as well as on the implications of that. Some of the generally agreed views regarding the consequences of this election roughly consist of the following: with the re-election of Cai, the Democratic Progressive Party (DPP) would be more confident now in its attempt to seek Taiwan independence; the current Taiwan government will be likely to adopt more provocative policies and measures to counter the influence of the mainland China; then the Chinese authority in response would take even tougher measures to limit Taiwan's activities at both regional and international levels; and the Cross-strait relations could risk being worsened.

Based on the understanding to some of the analysis, this piece would add a point that voting for Cai doesn't mean support of Taiwan independence, particularly, in Taiwan's case this time.

Taiwan locals didn't appear to be having another better choice for the time being. It is believed that a large number of Taiwan local people who are supportive of Taiwan-mainland unification still voted for Cai this time, mainly because the internal disunity of the Nationalist Party (KMT) - the main competitor of the DPP - offered a better chance for the DPP to win. The internal division of the KMT weakened the party's strength and position in running a good campaign, in bringing people together, and in leading Taiwan forward. At least at the present stage, the DPP appears to be more active in managing people's mood to make some Taiwan people believe that the DPP is more capable in leading. There is no doubt that people would usually vote for a stronger, more capable, and more united party rather than for a weaker and divided party.

Under the current circumstance, what could be the next for relevant sides – the KMT, the DPP, and the mainland then?

There is a necessity for the KMT to promote reform, including re-defining the party's position and direction, and allowing younger people within the party to get on the stage to inject more energy, strength and ideas into the party, in order to restore the confidence of the party.

For the DPP as well as for other parties, misperceptions of public opinions would be detrimental to both the parties and Taiwan. Wining an election is just of a temporary matter. Historical facts should be respected. Some wishful thinking should be avoided.

It is assumed that some people in Taiwan might have been influenced by the UK's exit from the European Union, and thought that Taiwan can also seek independence. For those having this kind of wishful thinking, they should be reminded that Taiwan's case is different from that of any other countries, given the fact that Taiwan is not a country, and any issue related to Taiwan is China's internal affairs.

In the case of the UK, it is an independent country. Leaving the European Union could mean a brighter future for it. By taking into account the UK's strength and influence, leaving the EU could also relate to a matter of contributing to the restructuring of the regional and international systems. In contrast, Taiwan is not recognized as a country both regionally and internationally. Seeking Taiwan independence has no future for Taiwan and the Taiwan people.

In addition to that, there could be other range of wishful thinking among a certain group of people in Taiwan as well — Some would expect to expand Taiwan's acting space and lift Taiwan's regional and international status by aligning with and relying on the United States; Some would believe that once a conflict takes place between the mainland and Taiwan, the U.S. would come to Taiwan's assistance to counter the mainland, because from the traditional geopolitical perspective, Taiwan appears to have a strategic significance to the U.S., because of which, the U.S. will not give up Taiwan; and Some in Taiwan may tend to seek a leverage between the U.S. and the mainland, and to take advantage of the growing competition between the two great powers.

All those wishful perceptions would be harmful to both Taiwan and the people there. The following part would respond to these kinds of thinking by listing a series of facts and analysis.

The U.S. was ever of a strong supporter to the KMT- led China in history. After the KMT lost control in the Chinese civil war, the U.S. stopped aiding to the KMT; then the commander of the KMT fled to Taiwan. Historical facts can tell that the cost of the U.S. support to the KMT was huge, yet it ended with the failure of the KMT and of the U.S. policy.

The U.S. and Taiwan were in a diplomatic relationship for more than 20 years before the then U.S. government and the then Chinese authority in late 1960s and early 1970s had made a series of grand moves to interact with each other; later in 1979 the two governments' joint efforts successfully led to the establishment of diplomatic relations between the two powers. Around the similar period of time, international voices of supporting the mainland were growing higher and higher, as a result of that, Taiwan-represented China in 1971 was removed out of the United Nations membership.

Obviously, the U.S. was aware that it wasn't in its interest to ignore the mainland while continuing to keep a diplomatic relationship with Taiwan, partly due to the U.S. necessity in implementing its cold war policy, and also to the fact that the then U.S. politicians saw a greater potential of cooperating with the mainland in a much longer term and from a wide range of aspects.

It is believed that all countries including the U.S. would take the interests of their nations and of their people as a very important matter. The U.S. wouldn't sacrifice the interests of its nation and of its people to aid Taiwan without limits. It didn't do that in the past, and neither would it do it in the new century. The cooperation, engagement and competition between the U.S. and China have never ceased to exist since decades ago. These will be likely to continue in the coming years, though the degree of competition and cooperation might be diverse occasion by occasion and in different stages. Overall, the benefits out of cooperation and engagement between China and the U.S. over the past years have never stopped growing; and the general trend that the two countries would make efforts to move this relationship forward and keep their competition on a controllable level will not likely alter in the foreseeable future.

Therefore, for those in Taiwan having some wishful thinking, as just analysed above, there should be a need for them to re-think carefully of the final consequences. Taiwan is not the KMT's Taiwan, neither is it the DPP's or any other parties' Taiwan. Taiwan is of people's Taiwan, and of China's Taiwan. Taiwan's future relies on a peaceful, stable, and prosperous One China.

As for other parties, it is seen in Taiwan the rising of other parties, whose propositions appear to be contrary to that of the DPP. There could be an opportunity for other political parties to play a role as well in the future. All the individuals, organizations, groups, and parties which are committed to promoting unification and leading Taiwan toward a better future should be encouraged and supported.

Over the past decades, Taiwan has benefited from the mainland dramatically more in economic and business terms, In the coming years, it is advisable for the two sides to deepen cooperation on other variety of issues such as people to people exchanges, joint cultural promotion activities, regular communications and discussions among think tanks, academic institutes, enterprises, and the media, as well as more exchanges in education etc. The Chinese authority may take into account whether there is a need to set up a series of mechanisms to regularly facilitate the exchanges and cooperation on those areas of issues. These types of activities are expected to lead to a better understanding between the mainland and Taiwan.

II. Moves of the United States on the Taiwan Issue under the Trump Administration: Symbolic or Substantial?

Over the past few months, the United States has taken a series of moves concerning the Taiwan issue – at the beginning of March, the U.S congress passed a "Taipei Act of 2019", through which, the U.S. described Taiwan as a close ally and pledged to further strengthen ties with Taiwan. Then, the U.S. leadership, more recently, has declared to deepen ties with Taiwan, and to assist Taiwan to expand its acting space at both regional and international levels. Further, upon the Taiwan local leader's inauguration for her second term on 20 May, the U.S. Secretary of State delivered a congratulatory message to Cai, and claimed that Taiwan remains as a strong and reliable partner of the United States. In the meantime, the U.S. government has notified the congress for a possible new arms sale deal with Taiwan worth of around $180 million.

Along with these series of actions taken by the U.S., here a number of questions raised are worth thinking about? - How do we see the nature and impact of these moves? More precisely, do they carry more of a symbolic meaning or of a substantial purpose? How could these actions possibly affect the policy direction of relevant political parties in Taiwan mainly including the Nationalist Party (KMT), the Democratic Progressive Party (DPP), and the New Party? How will the Cross-Strait relations will be like under Cai's new term? What should be the right future for Taiwan and for the relevant political parties in Taiwan from a long-term perspective? And what should be the wise choice for the U.S. and China concerning the Taiwan issue, as well as the China-U.S. bilateral relations and beyond from a long-term perspective?

How to Understand the Moves of the United States on Taiwan?

There have been a lot of discussions going on regarding some of the questions above. Some think that the recent moves taken by the U.S. on Taiwan are both symbolic and substantial. This analytical piece would share a view that they are more symbolic than substantial, as the reality is that the U.S. - Taiwan ties cannot move up further beyond the current stage in substantial terms, otherwise, it would risk a real conflict with the mainland, and a real war is not in the interest of all parties concerned.

Saying these moves symbolic is because they can be seen as a signal sent by the U.S. to the political parties in Taiwan, to the Taiwan public, as well as to the U.S. allies and other relevant countries across the globe. By doing so, the U.S. tends to show to the world that the United States should still be a reliable partner, and it is committed to protecting the interests of the U.S. and of its allies.

The period of the past recent months has been a very critical time for the U.S.. Amid the threat of the Coronavirus, the U.S. government's reputation, due to its way in handling the pandemic, has been seriously damaged both domestically and internationally. Hence, the U.S. must have to act in a seemingly very strong manner in order to remain confident. Besides that, acting strongly on foreign issues might aim to serve the U.S. election purpose.

On the Taiwan issue, while having made a lot of attempts to play the Taiwan card to balance the Mainland, the U.S. has also calculated its relations with both the Mainland and Taiwan very carefully in general terms, because the U.S. decision-makers know the bottom line concerning the Taiwan issue very well, which is that the Chinese government would never compromise on the issue of sovereignty.

Another point that needs to take into account when trying to understand the messages sent by the U.S. officials is that the U.S. is a liberal society, within which, different voices coming up from various officials at the same time shouldn't be a surprising matter. In other words, talking could be one thing, yet doing could be another thing sometimes from a democratic sense, especially in a liberal society, as the world has seen.

Impacts of the Series of Moves Taken by the U.S. Officials

Even though the U.S. does have no intention to pursue anything particularly substantial, the messages delivered by the U.S. officials could still cause an impact more or less on the political parties in Taiwan, in particular, on the DPP. More precisely, these could lead the Cai government to re-affirm its current hostile stance and policies toward the Mainland China, and encourage the DPP to seek even more ambitious plans to create problems in Cross-Strait relations. In Cai's inauguration speech on 20 May, she pledged to actively increase Taiwan's participation in regional cooperation mechanisms, and to raise Taiwan's role in contributing to peace, stability, and prosperity in the Indo-pacific region. Obviously, Cai's message reveals the Cai government's willingness to accommodate the U.S. Indo-pacific strategy. Also, the DPP sees bringing the U.S. in as a good opportunity to help highlight Taiwan's status. Nevertheless, this kind of attempts will be unlikely to make any breakthroughs, as far as the Cross-Strait relations remains in a difficult situation. Over all, the DPP's policies on the Mainland as well as on the U.S. under Cai's new term wouldn't expect to have dramatic changes.

For the New Political Party in Taiwan, the moves taken by the U.S. wouldn't likely cause a big impact on the policy direction of the New Party. The New Party maintains a stance of seeking unification with the Mainland. Its role will be expected to keep growing in the coming years in its relevance to promoting unification.

As for the KMT, right now it faces a series of critical choices in particular with regard to what policy direction the party should lead to, how to restore the unity of the party, and how to regain the public trust etc. After having suffered a range of serious losses, the KMT is in a stage of reforming and restructuring itself. The KMT at the moment doesn't seem to be quite certain about what policies the party should take. Under this circumstance, we shouldn't deny that the U.S. policies and moves could generate a detrimental impact on the KMP particularly in relation to the party's efforts in promoting unity. This analytical piece meanwhile would share a few points regarding this as follows.

In order to restore unity, confidence, and competitiveness, the most serious mistake the KMT should avoid making is to follow the DPP's policy direction. If the KMT chooses to follow the DPP's path, the chances for regaining unity and competitiveness would be lost, and the KMT's position would be further weakened.

The most important task for the KMT's reform at the current stage is to clear its stance and direction, and then only by constantly adhering to which, the party would have a future. The old and obscure stance, which has long been held by the KMT, is suggested to be abandoned. One of the former KMT leaders, regarding the Taiwan issue, ever held a position of "not seeking independence, not pursuing unification, and not resorting to force" (不独，不统，不武). Such kind of description is very obscure. What does this mean? It is purposely to keep Taiwan in a safe position as far as Taiwan doesn't directly seek independence. However, it also equals to the reality that Taiwan will remain in an independent status as long as it can.

From a long-term perspective, obscure stances should be detrimental to the future of the KMT and of Taiwan. It is time for the KMT to hold highly of the banner of seeking unification. The founding father of the KMT never wanted China to fall apart. An ever KMT - led China never wanted China to be separated. Unification is the most reliable goal for the KMT and for Taiwan. By working together with all other political parties, groups, organizations, and individuals who are supportive of this just undertaking toward that goal, Taiwan's fate as "a floating little boat in the middle of the sea" will be ended.

Selfish, expedient, and short-sighted vision for the purpose of winning a temporary election shouldn't have a place in the process of promoting the party's reform. To finally achieve the long-term goal of unification, the KMT is in need to work closely with other political parties which support a right course of promoting unification, as well as with all other just and positive forces in Taiwan. All these great efforts to be made by the KMT would be conducive to its current reform objective of restoring the unity of the party, of enhancing the party's capacity, of raising the party's profile, and of winning the people's trust.

In addition to that, most importantly, the KMT is suggested to deepen cooperation and dialogue with the Chinese authority, as well as to help facilitate exchanges and cooperation between the mainland and Taiwan from a wide variety of circles. Currently, the "1992 Consensus" serves as the political foundation for facilitating dialogue between the KMT and the Chinese authority. It is in need for the two sides to jointly work on more concrete measures toward unification. The signing of a new consensus might need to be taken into account. It is advisable for the Chinese authority and the KMT, with the support and participation of other relevant political parties, to refine the "1992 Consensus" by adding more concrete substances into it – such as the procedures, steps, measures, and other series of elements which could pave the way for jointly promoting unification. Before achieving the above, the "1992 Consensus" should still matter the most in bridging the Cross-strait dialogue and cooperation. Unification is a great undertaking supported by all those who respect historical facts and historical trend, and believe in human justice.

A Wise Choice for A Healthy China-U.S. Relations and Beyond

For the U.S. position on the Taiwan issue, the U.S. appears to have dragged itself into a dilemmatic situation – on the one hand, it recognized the government of the People's Republic of China as the sole legitimate authority representing the One-China; on the other hand, it keeps playing the Taiwan card to balance the Mainland. After all, the U.S. dilemmatic position is caused by its fear of losing balance, and of losing its number one great power status.

This kind of balancing tactic is reflective of one of the typical principles held by the realist school of thought-balance of power. In accordance with the realist tradition, the U.S. sees China as a competitor, in a way just like how the then great powers in history had seen each other. Yet, the U.S. judgment on China and China's policies could be wrong. The relevant assumptions could be mentally formed by certain politicians and policy advisers. The misjudgments among countries could lead to huge consequences. As history has told, a great number of conflicts were caused by misjudgments among states.

Balance of power, as one of the key principles of the realist tradition, was created to help maintain peace and prevent wars through balancing the power relations. In practice, it can be applied by developing alliance relationships among states. However, in history, the balance of power had always failed to prevent conflicts, mostly because the precondition for applying the balance of power strategy is that states usually have to hold a hostile attitude toward their counterparts; and they are suspicious of each other's intentions. The purpose of balancing is to contain the growing power of a particular state. In this case, as far as the hostile position of states is predefined, how could be possible for them to develop a peaceful relationship?

In addition to that, in line with the realist tradition, the alliance relationship is not necessarily to remain stable and reliable. By looking back at what had happened in history, great powers had frequently switched their alliance relationships from one to another in different historical periods. Therefore, it appears that the alliance relationship mostly carries an expedient purpose for states to protect their interests, and it doesn't usually and necessarily mean friendship among states.

After all, as being influenced by the realist tradition, it is no surprising that there could be misunderstandings between China and the U.S on certain regional and international issues. Apart from that, their differences in culture, philosophy, history, and development processes etc. might also play a part in contributing to certain misunderstandings between the two countries. As constructivism maintained, these factors matter a lot in terms of affecting the way how different states would deal with their counterparts.

On the Taiwan issue, the U.S. sees it more from a geopolitical and realist perspective, while China sees it more from a sovereign sense; the Chinese culture and tradition will not allow Taiwan to be separated from China. The Chinese development and civilization process in ancient times had been mostly driven by China's constant efforts to seek exchanges and cooperation with foreign powers. The ancient Silk Road should be a very good example to exhibit a basic fact that China had usually attempted to protect itself by seeking peaceful coexistence and collaboration with foreign powers, rather than by occupying and containing any other powers. For a very long historical period of time before the 19th century, China had been the most powerful and prosperous country in the world, yet the ancient Chinese power had treated foreign powers differently from the way that how other great powers in history had managed others.

By understanding well of the cultural and philosophical roots of the Chinese foreign policy, it should be easy to see that the Chinese foreign policy and military force in both ancient times and the modern era mostly carry a defensive rather than an offensive purpose. Therefore, in order to ensure a sound development of the China-U.S. bilateral relations in a long term as well as to help sustain a long-lasting peace in the Asia-pacific region and beyond, there is a strong necessity for the U.S. to rethink of its foreign policy, which has mainly been driven by a realist tradition, toward China; and it is also in need for the U.S. to respect China's legitimate right in pursuing unification, rather than create trouble between Taiwan and the Mainland.

III. Commentary: A Public Opinion Poll and Its Relevance to the Future Cross-strait Relations

In mid-August, an opinion poll concerning the future development of the Cross-strait relations released by the *Chinatimes* shown that the mainstream public opinion in Taiwan is supportive of the strengthening exchanges and communication between Taiwan and the Mainland. Generally younger generations having participated in the survey appeared to be more active and positive toward a closer engagement between Taiwan and the Mainland, with 72.4% of the young people aged between 20 and 29, and over 60% of those in the age group ranging from 30 to 49 supporting this idea.

Given the growing complex environment within Taiwan and at the regional and international stages, as well as the uneasiness of the Cross-strait relations at the moment, what could this opinion poll tell then? And what should be the main factor to have undermined people's efforts in promoting unification between the Mainland and Taiwan?

Roughly the public opinion poll could have revealed the following pieces of information: First, people in Taiwan, like all others from elsewhere in the world, anticipate a stable and secure living environment and a better quality of life, and they don't want wars and conflicts; second, the survey result apparently confronts some of the misleading claims such as "pro - the Mainland means selling Taiwan"; third, it uncovers a very important fact that the real problem having undermined people's efforts in promoting unification does not lie in the people themselves, rather, it lies in certain group of people especially some politicians in Taiwan - more precisely, the real problem lies in whether there are any politicians in Taiwan who have the conviction, capacity, and willingness to lead the people in Taiwan toward unification with the Mainland.

Certain Taiwan-independence forces have attempted to rouse the public mood against the Mainland by misleading the public to believe that the Mainland narrowed Taiwan's development space, and should be blamed for the possible worsening economic situation in Taiwan, while, in the meantime, having attempted to blur the root cause why the Mainland has limited Taiwan's acting space.

In the above case, the Taiwan-independence forces and some politicians acted mainly as a matter of their own interests, rather than of the interests of both Taiwan and the Taiwan people.

People's expectations have roughly been the same - they want a secure living environment and a better quality of life, and enjoy good education etc. Closer engagement and communication with the Mainland toward unification should be the best and most reliable approach to help meet the expectations of the Taiwan people, as well as for the Taiwan Island to have a long-term stability and prosperity.

As far as the people in Taiwan will be able to have a better and secure future through unification with the Mainland; and most importantly, the Mainland and Taiwan enjoy the same history, culture, and some good traditions, there should be no big point for them not to seek unification.

However, the current situation in Taiwan is that certain group of politicians and forces have constantly attempted to mislead the public and drive Taiwan toward a wrong direction by cutting the linkages between Taiwan and the Mainland in cultural and historical terms in particular.

Unfortunately for these forces, even though they have tried hard to misdirect the public, the mainstream public opinion poll once again proved the failure of their attempts.

Then this piece couldn't help to raise this question - which kind of leadership Taiwan and the Taiwan people need in order to overcome the above obstacles that have undermined people's efforts in seeking unification?

Apparently, the people need a capable leader as well as a group of competent team members. This group of people should be able to bring people hope, accommodate people's needs, and jointly shoulder the responsibilities of leading Taiwan toward the right path of seeking unification. Simply put, Taiwan and the Taiwan people need a leader and some competent people who will be able to make history together with the Mainland.

In addition to that, the unification of Taiwan and the Mainland will also greatly rely on the active participation of the current young generations from both Taiwan and the Mainland. The survey result uncovered that younger generations generally hold a more active and positive attitude to the deepening engagement and communication between the Mainland and Taiwan, and appear to be more open-minded toward the changes in today's world. They will be expected to bear more responsibilities in promoting closer exchanges and communication in all range of areas between the Mainland and Taiwan, and further in contributing to the great course of unification.

IV. Commentary: China's National Security Law and the Practice of the "One Country, Two Systems" Principle in Hong Kong

On 30 June, the Standing Committee of the National People's Congress of China passed the Law on Safeguarding National Security in the Hong Kong Special Administrative Region (HKSAR), and the law also came into force on the same day. In a reception held on 1 July to commemorate Hong Kong's return to the motherland 23 years ago, Hong Kong Chief Executive said that "the enactment of the national law is regarded as the most significant development in the relationship between the Central Authorities and the HKSAR since Hong Kong's return to the Motherland. It is a historical step to improve the system for Hong Kong to safeguard our country's sovereignty, territorial integrity and security. It is also an essential and timely decision for restoring stability in Hong Kong."[1]

It is believed that most of the Hong Kong residents would support the Hong Kong Chief Executive's points, and would agree that the promulgation of the National Security Law in Hong Kong is very significant and timely. For instance, in a

157

signing campaign, more than 3 million Hong Kong residents within 8 days had signed their names to show their strong support to the National Security Law.

The enactment of the National Security Law also received a strong international support. So far about 70 countries have expressed their support to the law, and opposed any foreign interference in China's internal affairs.

Meanwhile, a group of states have expressed their concern and criticized the enactment of the National Security Law in Hong Kong. The series of criticisms roughly centred on the following: the law violated the human rights and democratic freedoms of Hong Kong residents; and China tended to erode Hong Kong's autonomy by turning the "One Country, Two Systems" principle into the "One Country, One System" Principle etc. The U.S. House of Representatives in responding to this issue passed a "Hong Kong Autonomy Act"; and it threatened to take further measures against Hong Kong's interest. A couple of others within this group of states also pledged to receive more Hong Kong immigrants or allow the Hong Kong residents to seek asylum in their countries.

Overall, a lot of discussions and debates have been going on upon the promulgation of the National Security Law in Hong Kong. This analytical piece would add a brief point on the "One Country, Two Systems" principle, as well as share a view in responding to certain criticisms that the National Security Law violated the human rights and freedoms of Hong Kong residents.

About the "One Country, Two Systems" Principle

The "One Country, Two Systems" principle was designed and has been practised by China under a particular and critical historical condition. It is neither a commitment made by China to others, nor is it a treaty signed between China and others. In the very nature, the "One Country, Two Systems" principle is one of China's crucial national policies made by the Chinese government upon complex circumstances.

Apparently, the designing and adoption of the "One Country, Two Systems" policy was already reflective of the then Chinese policy makers' serious considerations of the Hong Kong local people's needs as well as of Hong Kong's special historical background. If without having taken these factors into account, upon Hong Kong's return to the motherland 23 years ago, China could have adopted a "One Country, One System" policy.

Hong Kong's autonomy status was empowered by China's Constitution many years ago. Setting up the Hong Kong Special Administrative Region, making and enacting the Hong Kong Basic Law, as well as establishing and practising the "One Country, Two Systems" principle all abide by the Constitution of the People's Republic of China. China, as an independent sovereign state, has every legitimate right and responsibility to adjust its national policies in order to better meet the people's needs as well as to well adapt to the changing internal and external situations. Other countries would do the same.

Whether the National Security Law Would Threat the Democratic Freedoms of Hong Kong Society?

As generally agreed among a wide range of circles, the National Security Law is to protect the practice of the "One Country, Two Systems", to safeguard national security, and to protect the interests, rights, and freedoms of majority of the people living in Hong Kong. Only those, who tend to break the law, threat national security, and deliberately offend the human rights, interests, and freedoms of the vast majority of ordinary Hong Kong residents through unlawful means, are fearful of the enactment of the National Security Law and see the law as a threat.

For the series of external forces who claimed to care about the human rights and democratic freedoms of the Hong Kong people, what they really care about seems to be their own interests, and what they obviously attempt to protect is the rights and freedoms of a small group of people who have either already committed a crime or have the potential to commit a crime. If this group of external forces are true human rights defenders, they are strongly suggested to listen to the voices of the majority of the Hong Kong residents.

Anyway, it is assumed that still the ideology may play a role behind the criticisms to the National Security Law. Some have tried very hard to defend the capitalist democratic system in Hong Kong, as they generally view that the capitalist democratic system is more advanced compared to other type of systems.

In response to those who still take the ideology as a big matter concerning Hong Kong and even beyond, this piece would suggest something as follows.

Ideology is an old issue having ever constrained the cooperation among nation states with different political and economic systems for a certain period of time. This ideological issue should be downplayed or abandoned when managing of relationship and collaboration among states in today's international relations.

There is a necessity for some to understand that Hong Kong's adoption of a capitalist system or of a socialist system in the future may not be the key to decide the areas of and levels of cooperation between Hong Kong and other countries. Whether the number of transnational groups, agencies, organizations, and corporations could continue to benefit from their collaboration with Hong Kong - as far as they abide by the law – will very much depend on what policies the Hong Kong local government will take, what polices the Chinese central government will take more crucially, whether China will be committed to deepening its reform and opening-up policy, and whether the local and central governments will be capable of implementing certain policies.

China has a different political system from the developed nations, yet over the past years since the implementation of China's opening-up policy, ideological difference hasn't affected China's engagement and collaboration with both democracies and non-democracies - it has neither affected China's participation in globalization and international cooperation, nor has it constrained China's efforts in promoting multilateralism together with other states, and nor has it prevented China's contribution to global governance.

After all, different political systems shouldn't matter that much anymore, as long as countries, democracies or non-democracies, are really committed to finding out solutions to address the common challenges faced by the world today.

Notes

1.Quoted in a speech made by Hong Kong Chief Executive Carrie Lam in a reception to mark the 23rd anniversary of Hong Kong's return to the motherland. *China Daily.* 1 July 2020.

https://www.chinadailyasia.com/article/135410

Conclusion

The previous chapters of this book have assessed what have been happening on the global stage as well as between the two major powers, China and the United States. There were broad analysis and also detailed assessment on the range of issues concerning values and theories, global governance, globalization, China-U.S. engagements, the coronavirus, and others etc.

China-U.S. interactions would not only generate big impacts on the two countries but also on the world. Therefore, this book has put a heavy focus on exploring how China and the U.S. have engaged with each other over the past years; meanwhile, it has also tended to foresee the likely development of China-U.S. cooperation and competition in the future from a number of aspects mainly consisting of foreign and security affairs, economic and trade issues, technology, and global governance.

Apart from that, given the serious damage of the coronavirus to the world as well as the grave concerns attached by various countries to the pandemic, this research has mainly analysed the implications of the COVID-19 to people's daily lives, power relations, globalization, non-traditional security, and world order etc. Presumably, the repercussions caused by the pandemic will last for some years to come; and it might add more uncertainties to global economic recovery, global governance, and major power relations etc.

This book has also touched on issues related to Taiwan and Hong Kong. 2020 was a significant year for both Taiwan and Hong Kong - Taiwan held a new local election; the year of 2020 also witnessed the promulgation of the National Security Law in Hong Kong. Given what have been happening in Taiwan and Hong Kong over the past few years, and the numerous discussions and debates having been raised in the meantime, this project has tried to share some views in relation to the issue of Hong Kong and of Taiwan from an objective and historical perspective.

Anyway, in the coming years, new possibilities might emerge concerning the range of subjects examined in this book. This study hopefully can meet a purpose of promoting knowledge exchanges and facilitating more meaningful discussions; and more crucially, it is expected to contribute to problem-solving on the issues assessed in the book.

References

Biden Joe (2020). "An Interview to the U.S. President-elect Joe Biden by the New York Times". *Tecent.* 3 December 2020. http://finance.qq.com/a/20201203/000358.htm

Carri Lam (2020). "A speech made by Hong Kong Chief Executive Carrie Lam in a reception to mark the 23rd anniversary of Hong Kong's return to the motherland". *China Daily.* 1 July 2020. https://www.chinadailyasia.com/article/135410

Fukuyama Francis (2020). "Liberalism and Its Discontents: the Challenges from the Left and the Right". *American Purpose.* 5 October 2020. https://www.americanpurpose.com/articles/liberalism-and-its-discontent/

He Yafei (2015). *China's Historical Choice in Global Governance.* Renmin University Press.

General Administration of Customs of the People's Republic of China (2020). "Trade figures for the year of 2019 were released by the General Administration of Customs of the People's Republic of China". *Sohu.* 14 January 2020. http://www.sohu.com/a/366906629_557006

Ian Goldin (2013). *Divided Nations-Why Global Governance Is Failing, and What We Can Do about It.* Oxford University Press.

Kagan Donald (1969). *The Outbreak of the Peloponnesian War.* NY: Cornell University Press.

Kissinger Henry (2015). *World Order.* Penguin Books.

Kissinger Henry (2020). "An Interview to the U.S. former Secretary of State Dr. Henry Kissinger by the Bloomberg Editor-in-Chief John Micklethwait on 16 November 2020 upon an online convening of the New Economy Forum 2020". *The Paper.* 21 November 2020. http://www.thepaper.cn/newsDetail_forward_10089244

Kissinger Henry (2020). "The Coronavirus Pandemic Will Forever Alter the World Order". Remarks by Dr. Henry Kissinger originally released by *The Wall Street Journal* on 3 April 2020. *Xinjingbao.* https://baijiahao.baidu.com/s?id=1663314191540020269&wfr=spider&for=pc

Ministry of Commerce of the People's Republic of China (2019). "China-U.S. trade data for the year of 2018 was released by the Ministry of Commerce of the People's Republic of China during its Regular Press Conference on 17 January 2019". *Guancha.* 17 January 2019. http://www.guancha.cn/economy/2019_01_17_4

87276.shtml

Nye Joseph (2018). "American Leadership and the Future of the Liberal International Order". *China International Strategy Review 2018*. PP. 1-15

Nye Joseph (2000). *Understanding International Conflicts: An Introduction to Theory and History* (Third Edition). LONGMAN: An imprint of Addison Wesley Longman, Inc.

Thucydides (1972). *History of the Peloponnesian War*. London: Penguin.

Yao Yang (2020). "How to Understand the Dual Circulation of the Chinese Economy". *Sina.* 13 October 2020. finance.sina.com.cn/zl/china/2020-10-13/zl-iiznezxr5790402.shtml

The Author

Jin Ran is Founder and Director of the Centre for Strategic Thinking, which is a research and advisory think tank, committed to promoting knowledge sharing and problem-solving on core issues of regional and international concern.

****

The views appeared in this book are the author's. They don't represent those of the Centre for Strategic Thinking, or of any other agencies or institutions. In addition, this study bears no responsibility for the accuracy of the data cited from other academic works or relevant institutions.

CPSIA information can be obtained
at www.ICGtesting.com
Printed in the USA
BVHW041007301121
622865BV00018B/858